DIVINE SUPERNATURAL ENCOUNTERS

One Man's Journey with God

Donald D. Young

DIVINE SUPERNATURAL ENCOUNTERS

One Man's Journey with God

By Donald D. Young
Copyright © 2010 by Donald D. Young

www.NBSOS@.org
New Beginnings School of Spirit
is a 501c3 nonprofit organization

Printed by Dare2Dream Books
Pearland, TX 77584

All rights reserved. The copyright laws of the United States of America protect this book. The use of short quotations or occasional page copying for personal or group study is permitted unless otherwise identified. Scriptures quoted are from: the Holy Bible, New King James Version; New Living Translation, © Copyright 1996, 2004, permission given by Tyndale House Publishers. Wheaton, Illinois 60189 and from "The Message" Copyright © 1993, 1994, 1995, 1996, 2000, 2001, 2002; Used by permission of Nav Press Publishing Group. Emphasis within scripture quotations is the author's own. Please note that publishing style capitalizes certain pronouns in Scripture that refer to Father, Son, and Holy Spirit and may differ from some publishers' styles.

ISBN: 978-0-9779694-3-2

"DIVINE SUPERNATURAL ENCOUNTERS"

Table of Contents

Dedication

SECTION #1 ~ In the Beginning. 9
    The Womb or the Tomb
    The Nickel
    A Lost Cow
    Discouragement and Despair
    Radical Abandonment
    A Mental Renewing
    Exodus 3:2
    The Prayer Closet
    Hearing God at Unexpected Times

SECTION #2 ~ 1980. 44
    Forgiveness at Work
    Supernatural Help
    Drawing Closer
    Filled - Healed - Delivered
    An Appointed Day of Deliverance
    A Changed Man
    Marketing
    Questions Lead to Learning
    Prophetic Hunger
    Tongues & Interpretation

Brother Who
Supernatural Mark
Laying on of Hands
Bed Wetting
Witchcraft
Hidden Treasure
Time, Treasure & Talents
Fragrances
Set Free
An Exorcism
Christian Mystics
A Wooden Spoon
Daily Confessions
Open Heavens
The Shekinah Glory
Faith to Receive the Supernatural
Poland

SECTION #3 ~ 1992.......................139
    The Apartment
    Angelic Interventions
    A Trial with Sickness
    Growing in Experience
    10:40 PM
    Sweet Times of Learning
    Healed of a Fatal Disease
    Babysitting a Cat
    The Oil of Separation
    Malachi 3:16-18

The South Texas Adventure
Spiritual Forefathers
1 Kings 19:19
Divine Humor
Smiting the Enemy

SECTION #4 ~ 1996.........................197
Translated
A Prophetic Word
The Spirit of Truth
Time for Rest
Judgment
End Time Ministers
New Age
Eternity
A Cult
Barrenness
A Funeral
Levels of Demon Possessions
Surprised by an Angel
Airport Angels
Bible Reading
A Prophetic Token
15 Pounds in 15 Days
To be Full or a Fool
Meeting
Some Clarity
Word Curses
Spirit of Levitation

Candles
Snow Angels
The Hot Tub Adventure
A Name Change
Mark 2:22
A Knife
The Day of Atonement
A Word for You
A Final Attempt
Prayer Request
Know Those Who Labor Among You
Closing Prayer
Become a Partner
Back Of Book

Dedication

The dedication of this book is to my Lord and Savior who talks to me in out of the ordinary and extraordinary ways. I am so grateful that my heavenly Father has taken the time to communicate with me, even when I do not understand everything that is being said, and even when I am not listening for His still small voice. His voice sounds wonderful to me, no matter how I hear it. You are indeed an awesome God. You are the one I love totally and unconditionally.

I thank my wife, Karah, who kept encouraging me to write and most importantly rewrite. Your constant encouragement and faith in me to become the man that I am called to be in Christ, is what kept me pushing forward, not giving up on accomplishing this book. In addition, I want to thank my daughter Kariy, who kept encouraging me to keep believing that God would use this book to help others run the race of life. Thank you both for all the faithful seeds of encouragement you have sown into my life. The dedication of this book is also to all the saints who desire to have a lifestyle full of "Divine Supernatural Encounters" through Jesus Christ our Lord and Savior.

I Want To Encourage Every One Of You Do Not Ever Quit; Keep Asking, Seeking and Knocking For Divine Supernatural Encounters!

God loves His children to Ask, Seek, and Knock (A.S.K.) on the door of the supernatural. Over the years, I have learned God honors anyone who decides not to quit seeking Him. Humbling themselves before the Lord with prayer, study of His Word and fasting will help build the faith needed to enter into His precious prophetic promises and blessings that are waiting for the believer.

God has precious, prophetic, promises waiting for everyone who is willing to stay focused on the things He has preordained for them. These promises become our anchor of hope the moment we believe. We purify ourselves as we hope in Jesus, just as He is pure (1 John 3:3). It is up to each individual to prepare his or her own heart to be good ground, which will reproduce natural and spiritual fruit. Some will produce thirty–fold, some sixty–fold, and some will produce even a hundred–fold harvest as they submit to Gods living word as it walks through the garden of their heart in the cool of the day (Mark 4:20).

"Grace and peace be multiplied unto you through the knowledge of God, and of Jesus our Lord, according as his divine power hath given unto us all things that pertain unto life and godliness, through the knowledge of him that hath called us to glory and virtue. Whereby are given unto us exceeding great and precious promises: that by these ye might be partakers of the divine nature, having escaped the corruption that is in the world through lust" (2 Peter 1:2-4).

SECTION #1

In the Beginning

I have taken the liberty of repeating myself on several instances hoping to impart a better understanding on a topic or a spiritual occurrence. Repetition is one method of learning. Each time I repeated myself I expanded the teaching in its breadth, length, depth, or height (Ephesians 3:18). My desire is to help you dig your own well of knowledge and understanding.

A great deal of this book may cover prophetic events that you do not understand. Although you personally may not have experienced the spiritual mystical realm, that does not nullify its value.

God alone establishes principles. God has set into motion certain physical principles (laws, rules, statues and ordinances). The law of gravity is one example of God's natural laws. We cannot see gravity or touch it, but if you jump off the Empire State Building, you will come face to face with the dreadful cost of breaking such a law. Just because an individual does not understand the laws of gravity does not nullify its existence or importance. Therefore, whether you "believe" in gravity or deny its existence, the laws, rules, statues and ordinances of God still have final say over your life. The same is true with the supernatural things of God. Unbelief does not nullify the reality of the supernatural things of God.

I have taken the liberty to paraphrase a great deal of the scriptures as it relates to my story or the spiritual occurrence. At the end of many of the sentences, you will notice a bible verse text. I highly recommend you look up such verses to obtain greater clarity and understanding.

The Womb or the Tomb

My mother had so much sickness while I was in her womb that her Christian doctor offered her an abortion in the early months. She declined and resigned herself to the fact that she was going to have this child or die trying. We both made it and this is where my story begins.

Because of a difficult labor, my birth had extensive medical circumstances surrounding it; I was born a blue baby due to the lack of oxygen. It is interesting that blue is the color which symbolizes heavenly prophetic revelation? The physical conditions surrounding my birth actually pointed to the fact that I would become a prophetic minister in the Kingdom of God. I really do not think this could possibly be a coincidence. One of the many things I have learned during these past thirty-three years is that God has plans not only for me but also for everyone on planet earth. We will only enter into His plans for our life if we submit to His word, will and way on a daily basis. To everything, there is a season, a time for every purpose under heaven (Ecclesiastes 3). We must remember that the thief comes to steal, and to kill, and to destroy but Jesus came to give us life and that we might have it more abundantly (John 10:10).

Many believers do not realize the areas the devil steals, kills, and destroys in their life. The majority of the time they think of their car, job, money, or fun time's with friends and family members. You may want to consider other areas such as your faith, hope, love, righteousness, peace, wisdom, knowledge, favor, patience, kindness, goodness, faithfulness, gentleness, self-control, joy, understanding etc...

Jesus came to destroy the works of the enemy. Jesus came to bless these very same areas plus a thousand other things in a person's life. Jesus came to give us life more abundantly (Deuteronomy 1:11).

It is clear to see that what the enemy meant for evil God is continually turning it for my good. Due to the medical conditions surrounding my birth, I spent the first 30 days of my life in an incubator. This extensive length of time became the seedbed for additional medical problems. At that time, hospitals did not know that unregulated oxygen levels in incubators could cause other complications such as blindness or brain damage in many infants.

The unregulated oxygen caused both eyes to develop cataracts during infancy. At the age of five, I underwent five eye surgeries. At the age of six, I was able to see clearly for the very first time. Prior to those surgeries, I only knew familiar voices and shadows. Now I was able to function in society.

I do not believe my parents or my doctor considered what I would encounter in life due to the lack of unregulated oxygen. Because I did not die, my parents assumed that I would be like any other child. The doctors and my parents attributed my slowness during my developmental years to my blindness; however, as time went by, it was clear that I also had a learning disability.

My mother was the first to notice that I had "motor skill" problems. Upon entering school, she discovered that I also had extensive learning difficulties. During the fifties, the educational systems did not label a child as A.D.D. or dyslexic. Instead of saying that a child had a learning disability, they put the child in one of three categories, above normal, normal, or below normal. I was labeled at the bottom of the below normal grid. During my early years in school, no one seemed to make the connection between the difficulties surrounding my birth and my learning disabilities. It is now easy for me to understand that a large majority of childhood learning disabilities often revolve around the child's time in the womb and especially during the child's birth.

Because of these things, life never came easy for me. I always had a difficult time learning everything in school. The "show and tell" teaching format that is the easiest form of learning was difficult for me to understand. I did not retain anything that I had seen or heard for any length of time. By the time I had reached the age of ten, I had just finished the second grade for the second time. My parents made the choice to place me in a private Christian school. For the first seven years of my education, they felt by placing me in a private school, I would receive the additional help I needed, and I would eventually be able to live normal productive life.

The Nickel

It was a hot July day and I was sitting on the front porch when I spotted the old sway back horse pulling the ice cream wagon at the corner of our street. Although we were living in the city and all of our roads were paved with asphalt, the owner had chosen a horse drawn wagon to sell his summertime refreshments. I think it was more of a novelty idea because whether you purchased an ice cream or not, every child on our block came out to pet the horse; my favorite was the nickel ice cream sandwich. It was about three inches square and about an inch thick. The sandwich had a white cardboard edging that held the cream in place until it became frozen solid. That edging was always the last thing I would lick as I tried to get every little morsel of the frozen cream I could.

When I saw the ice cream wagon turn onto our street, I ran into my house and asked my mother for a nickel. She stopped washing dishes just long enough to say she did not have any money and if I wanted any ice cream I had to go outside and "dig up my own nickel."

With that in mind, I went out to the street and began to pace up and down in front of our house. Finally, I settled on a location and began to kick at the newly laid asphalt with the heel of my shoe. I kept looking down the street at the wagon, which was getting closer every moment. The closer he got the faster and harder I kicked at the asphalt. It was as if I was in a race to find a nickel before the wagon passed me by. Suddenly, a chuck of asphalt about the size of my hand flipped over, and went into the gutter. I looked down and there laid a shiny nickel. I picked it up, waved to the wagon driver to stop and bought myself an ice cream sandwich.

My shortcut to the back yard was to go in our front door and out the back door before mom could catch me. This day that did not work. When she saw me she asked, "How did you get that ice cream?" For a brief moment, I thought I was in big trouble because of the sound in her voice. With a trembling voice I said, "Mom I dug up a nickel just like you told me to go and do." She shook her head as she muttered something about children and motioned with her hand for me to get out of the house before the ice cream melted and made a mess.

That night when I went to bed, I thought about how I found that nickel. What was so interesting to me even as a young child was that this was not the first time something like this had happened to me! At times, I would dream of meeting someone and the next day, I would meet him or her. I never considered why this occurred in my life. To me it was normal and I thought everyone had these same types of experiences.

Learning did not come easy for me. I spent two years in the first grade and was now in the second grade for the second time. That same year, May 5, 1958, I became a Christian. I remember the day very well. I sat at my desk quietly, with tears streaming down my face. The teacher had just read a Bible story and offered prayer for anyone who wanted to receive salvation and go to heaven one day. This was the beginning of the first day of my life. Somehow, I had reached the conclusion that God had just called me and I had to respond or He might never call me again. I remembered sliding out of my seat and slowly walking to the front of the classroom. That is when I made a confession of faith in the Lord Jesus Christ. Kneeling next to my teacher's huge wooden desk, I recited the two most famous Bible verse known to man.

"For God so loved the world that he gave his only begotten Son, that whosoever believeth in him should not perish, but have everlasting life. For God sent not his Son into the world to condemn the world; but that the world through him might be saved" (John 3:16-17)

After I asked Jesus Christ to come into my heart, the teacher reached into the bottom drawer of her desk and took out a black King James pew Bible. Opening it to the front–page, she wrote my name, the date, and a note in green ink that I had become a Christian.

As a child, I probably had heard the gospel a thousand times. I possibly heard the gospel more than anyone else had in the entire world. I felt this way because I would hear one sermon after another when my family went to South Texas to visit my granddad's farm. My grandfather was bivocational: he was a farmer and a preacher. My mom constantly reminded me that I had a rich spiritual heritage. She told me how my grandparents went forth in a tent meeting and received salvation while attending a Smith Wigglesworth's meeting. I heard how grandpa and grandma followed Smith Wigglesworth around wherever he was preaching for several years after they received salvation. Sometimes he would remain at a location or a meeting for several weeks or even several months before moving on to his next location. When this occurred, my grandparents would stay at an individual's home they had met at the meeting. My granddad would do odd jobs during the day and attend the meetings at night.

After years of following Smith Wigglesworth around my grandparents settled down and purchased a boarding house on the outskirts of Toronto, Canada. That was where they became acquainted with another minister, Amie Semple McPherson. She rented a room at grandmother's boarding house. As it turned out, once a week, Pastor Amie would have a prayer meeting and grandmother would play the piano and lead worship. Over the years I heard countless stories of deliverances, miracles, healings and many salvations that occurred when Pastor Amie ministered in that boarding house.

Although I had asked Jesus Christ into my heart, I did not feel I was living for Him. I was not committed to Jesus Christ and was only giving Him lip service. Since I did not really have a special experience or a living relationship with Jesus, these stories made absolutely no sense to me. For years, all I did was draw near to God with my mouth and did not honour him. I had no fear of God in my life (Isaiah 29:13).

Mother told how my grandparents had finally obtained citizenship in America, and eventually moved to Arkansas, where Grandpa attended a Pentecostal Church School. After spending two years in school, they moved to South Texas to a twenty–acre farm, which they had purchased while living in Canada.

My grandparents lived on the farm while my mom was growing up. For over fifty years, they farmed and preached. When they both begin to suffer from poor health, they moved in with my parents. After my grandmother passed away, I began to spend a large amount of time with my granddad.

A Lost Cow

When not in school, I spent most of my days working at my family's plumbing shop. I worked weekends and summers when I was not attending summer school. Most of the time, I did not get much playtime, but when I did, oh boy, look out! As boys often do, several of us were well on our way to getting into some trouble on a daily basis. I know when you get a group of boy's together one thing leads to another. I was always trying to look cool in front of my friends. I actually did my best to avoid trouble because I feared my mom and God— in that order. Mom would always tell me just before giving me a spanking, "I am doing this because God said for me to do it." I did not have the correct understanding of God and His love as a young boy.

One day as we were playing with matches in the playhouse, I noticed the toes of my granddad's brown shoes on the other side of a curtain that hung in the doorway. The moment I saw those shoes I knew I was in big trouble. Fear swept through my entire body because I knew I was not to play with matches. I looked out the little window but saw no one. I ran outside to separate myself from the possibility of getting into more trouble. To my surprise, my granddad was nowhere in sight. I ran into the house and asked my mom where granddad was. Without even looking up, she said, "Daddy has been in the back bedroom all day reading his Bible and praying." From that day on, I began to wonder what happened. How could he read his Bible, pray, and be in the back yard checking on me all at the same time? Our house had two doors, the front and the back door. Mom would have noticed granddad if he had left the house. Now I know God had given me a vision of granddads shoes to bring me to my senses.

It was evident to everyone that my mom was extremely proud of her father. She constantly reminded me that granddad was a prophet. Mom told me how granddad would pray four to six hours a day in preparing for a meeting. When she began to reminisce about growing up, she would talk about the hand full of creative miracles God did through granddad. Mom told the same stories to every neighbor who would stand still long enough to listen. One particular story she told was about a neighbor who asked granddad to seek God to find his lost cow. No one could remember a time when granddad did not see exactly where to find lost livestock. It was very similar to when Saul went to Samuel, the seer, to find where his father's asses had wondered off three days prior (1 Samuel 9:8, 19-20). Unfortunately, no one gave granddad a piece of silver like the one Samuel received for telling where to find the lost livestock.

I enjoyed Granddad living with us and looked forward to our daily visits. Every day I had homework and had to dig ditches for the plumbing company. I quickly learned if I did not have my studies completed, I would not have to dig ditches and could stay at home with granddad. I often put off my studies while mom was at work and did them at night, leaving me plenty of time to visit with granddad. I was very pleased with myself and enjoyed sitting daily on the back porch visiting with granddad. Every time I would get around him, he would place one hand on my head, hold his Bible in the other hand and pray in other tongues for at least an hour. The first time I heard him speak in other tongues it amazed me. It sounded great although I did not know what he was saying. As strange as it might sound, this did not really bother me at all. I loved the positive attention granddad gave me. After praying in other tongues, he would pray with understanding, which then led to prophesying for ten or fifteen minutes. I wished I had paid closer attention to his prayers and prophetic words. Because of my great love for him, I chose sitting with granddad instead of playing.

Every time granddad prayed with his hand on my head, it felt as if fire was falling through my entire body. The first time this occurred, I remember jumping off the stool I was sitting on. That experience frightened me so much that it was several days later before I allowed him to pray for me again.

Over time, I became accustomed to his long prayers along with the fire falling through my body, and other manifestations. Once I asked him why he prayed over me so much. He said, "Because you are the first-born and all males that open the womb belong to the Lord God. They are consecrated, sanctified and holy unto the Lord set apart at birth for His work" (Exodus 13:2; Luke 2:23). He would tell me "about a special call on my life" as he mentioned the "Supernatural Mark" that was on the top of my head at birth. "The Mark" was a dark blue and purple six-pointed star with Hebrew writing in it. Then, he would always end by saying; "God does not choose everyone although He calls many" (Matthew 22:14).

I always felt a special peace when I was around my granddad. I realize now I was sensing a special anointing from God that rested upon him. Mother often told me others referred to granddad as "A Peace Maker" (Matthew 5:9).

This meant that the spirit of peace was always present. I knew that my granddad could walk up and say "hello" to a total stranger and they would follow him around like a little puppy. Mom referred to this as a charismatic anointing, like an invisible force that draws people. If they lingered for any time at all, he was going to quote the "Romans Road" to them. He never stopped talking with a person, without giving them an opportunity to accept Christ as their personal Savior. If they were a believer, he would ask if they wanted to rededicate their life to Jesus Christ. When I was fourteen, my granddad died. His death was one of my greatest losses. Because of the love I had for him, it took nearly a year before I could go out on the back porch without tears coming to my eyes. Granddad's favorite cliché comes to mind: "Remember the highway to hell is paved with good intentions. Duane you only enter through the narrow gate; for the gate is wide and the way is broad that leads to destruction, and there are many who enter through it" (Matthew 7:13).

Discouragement and Despair

I constantly lagged behind my peers because of failing grades. I attended summer school every year due to my inability to comprehend and retain what I had learned no matter how hard I tried. In 1969, I finally graduated from high school at the age of twenty–one through many great struggles.

I do not remember a day in school that I did not face discouragement. I wanted to quit school many times. Each time my mom encouraged me to hang in there and graduate. English, reading comprehension, and grammar, were foundational subjects that I struggled with and disliked the most. Every student in one English class was required to give an oral report; I do not know why I feared public speaking so much but I would physically shake and stutter when required to speak in front of a group. My oral report was so poorly delivered I would always get a failing grade because no one could understand what I was trying to express. My reading and retention skills were so poor that by the age of thirty, I had not read twenty-five books including schoolbooks in my entire life. I am not proud of this fact. I want you to understand, I was illiterate in many areas. I share my story so you will understand that what God has done for me is truly a miracle. In addition, He will do the same for anyone who will pursue Him and His great love. Every good gift and perfect gift is from above, and comes down from the Father of lights, who has no variableness, neither is there a shadow of His turning (James 1:14).

During my teen years, dad told me so many WWII stories I began looking forward to joining the Air Force, which was the main reason I wanted to graduate from high school. The day after I graduated, I was standing at the Air Force Recruiter's office when they opened the doors. Within a few minutes, I had signed on the dotted line and three days later was heading to a nearby Air Force Base for my physical.

I had stayed in school, graduated, and had a sense of accomplishment for the first time in my entire life "Yes, I have finally made it." I returned to the Air Force recruiter's office after finding a draft notice in the mail. I was worried that the Army would get me and I would not realize my dream. The recruiter assured me all was ok since I had signed up with the Air Force before receiving the letter. There were eight of us on our way to the base. I remember that entire day as if it were yesterday. I was a little bit anxious, but the joy and excitement of joining the Air Force squashed any feelings I had of anxiousness.

I was just one of several thousand young men taking the physical that day. We formed a long single line, moving from one doctor to another doctor, all day long. My adrenalin was off the chart I could hardly contain myself. I could not believe this wonderful day that I had dreamed for so many years had finally happened.

Everything was going fine, until I stood before their eye specialist; that was when my balloon burst. Shaking his head the eye doctor said, "Young man, you are not eligible for any branch of the Unites States Armed Forces" as he continued to reassure me it was not a disgrace to have failed the eye examine.

I explained I did not want to pilot an airplane I just wanted to be in the United States Air Force. I told him that the Air Force has over 20,000 different jobs available from which an individual may choose. No matter what I said, he would not listen. I was speechless as I was ushered into a waiting room.

As I waited in the release room, a second doctor came in and told me that I did not make the minimum required score on the mental exam. Once again, I was crushed; I regretted my life as well as ever being born. I felt like all the efforts and struggles I had endured were for nothing.

The ride back to my hometown was miserable. The recruiter kept switching from one radio station to another in hopes of finding a joyful sound. For the return trip, I picked a seat in the far back of the van and sat quietly looking out into the dark lonely night as tears of self–pity streamed down both cheeks. As I stared into the night, I heard a voice, and for a fleeting moment it was so loud I thought someone had spoken audibly. I soon realized the voice must have been in my mind. Years later, I came to realize it was the inward voice of the Holy Spirit. The voice said, "Son, you will become a soldier in a spiritual army. I have not rejected you." Even with that declaration, I did not feel better. I continued to stare out into the dark night as we traveled down the highway for the three hour ride home. I began to wonder if I was losing my mind. I do not think I had ever felt this disappointed in my entire life. I was almost numb. Little did I realize that one day I would be in the army of the Lord!

Although I hated my job with a passion, I had become a third generation plumber, working at my family's business. Because the plumbing trade was "hands on" and did not require much knowledge, I knew it very well. Although I worked hard and made good money, plumbing did not fulfill the greatest desires of my heart. Unfortunately, I did not know what those desires were anymore. I had missed my lifelong goal and the desire to aspire to anything was gone. The only thing in my heart during those years was sin, and I knew it too well. I tried everything I could to find joy and never did experience it. Hunting, fishing, drinking, and partying left me with the same old empty feelings. Nothing produced any form of lasting joy. My heart was empty and I lived a constant life of discouragement and despair. It was only by the grace of God that I never got into the drug scene. Sometimes, when I really got down on myself, I would remember when I said the sinner's prayer and remind myself that one day everything would be ok. I often thought about the verse which says, "There is none righteous, no, not one for we all have sinned and fall short of the glory of God" (Romans 3:10, 23).

I kept telling myself that everyone sins, and that there was no way to keep from sinning. Little did I realize that I did not have to sin. That theology is a lie straight from the pit of hell. The Bible calls this theology the "doctrines of demons." The apostle Paul gave us a warning concerning Satan's doctrine.

"Now the Spirit speaketh expressly, that in the latter times some shall depart om the faith, giving heed to seducing spirits, and doctrines of devils; Speaking lies in hypocrisy; having their conscience seared with a hot iron" (1 Timothy 4:1-2).

I was a great sales representative for my family's business; my dad said I was so good I could sell ice cubes to an Eskimo! Although I had developed the reputation of a great sales representative, money and promotion still did not produce joy. Inside, it felt as if I was missing something but I did not know what. A friend took me to a motivational meeting that was uplifting but did nothing for my inward, empty feeling. I left that meeting in the same condition as I had arrived "empty." It was as if a black cloud of discouragement and despair constantly followed me around. It was several years later before I discovered that my joy only comes from one person and that person is Jesus Christ. His joy will remain within anyone who wants it enough to pursue it (John 15:11).

Radical Abandonment

Between twenty one and thirty years old, my focus was on making lots of money—money had become my god! During those early years of owning my own business, I never once darkened a church door. I was in such a backslidden condition that I would not have made it into heaven if I had died during those years.

It was only by God's grace and possibly my grandparent's prayers that kept me alive. I was involved in over a dozen auto accidents, an explosion, as well as many other foolish job related accidents. I looked at everything from a financial standpoint. When I made decisions concerning my work or my family, I would evaluate what it was going to cost me. I wanted to know how much money I would put into my pocket. Somehow, I had reached the conclusion that if I made more money, I would be happier. That is a lie straight out of hell. Money does not bring happiness.

You do not have to be a millionaire to worship money. A poor person who has no money can worship the little money he or she has just as easily as a person who has much. I did not realize that I was in love with money and that its deep roots continually bombarded all that I did or thought (1 Timothy 6:10; Hebrews 13:5).

No one can keep the first commandment without surrendering all to Jesus. We are to love the Lord God with all our heart, all our soul and all our body (Matthew 22:37). We give our time, treasure and talents to earn the money we have. This is the reason the Bibles says so much about money. Until God has our all, He has received nothing at all. You can give God your money and still not yield yourself to Him. However, you cannot fully surrender your all to Him without also surrendering your money. I knew I was neither honoring nor worshiping God at all, but God's loving mercy was about to change my life forever.

My oldest daughter had accepted Christ and I had agreed to watch her receive water baptism. At that time, this was something I personally had never done.

As soon as I entered the church, I sat down on the very back pew closest to the door. Because I was a first time visitor, the pastor wasted no time in taking advantage of my visit. He preached a real "Hell, Fire, and Brimstone Message," which kept me squirming in my pew during the entire service. When the pastor gave the alter call I held on to the pew in front of me so tightly that my knuckles began turning white. A deacon came up behind me and tapped me on the shoulder as the choir sang the song "Just As I am" for the fifth straight time. When he tapped me, I jumped and began to tremble. I did not know why, but I remember feeling frightened and anxious. The usher leaned over and told me that my two youngest daughters had also gone forth to accept Christ. The pastor asked if I would come down and stand with them. I wasted no time in responding "NO" to his question.

I was glad when the service was over; I rushed out to my car. As I waited for my daughters to join me, I thought about how I felt while in the church. I did not know why I was so fearful. Nothing I heard that day made any sense to me.

It became more and more evident to me that I was not right with God. I was sweating as if someone had been chasing me for a city block. Earlier that week a neighbor had told me that God was angry with me because I was not going to church, which was another of the devils lies—called a doctrine of demons (1 Timothy 4). I remembered my granddad always told me that God is love and we could love Him because He first loved us (1 John 4).

Later that afternoon as I sat watching the evening news, I thought about the "Hell, Fire, and Brimstone Message." That sermon coupled with all the Godly sayings my granddad had deposited into my heart finally hit home. It was evident that I was under the convicting power of the Holy Spirit. I had always heard that the Holy Spirit gently nudged an individual's heart. That was not the case with me. It felt like the Holy Spirit had taken a ten-pound sledgehammer and was beating the hell out of me. I will have to admit; I had plenty of hell in me.

I went to bed, but could not sleep. I got up and rummaged around in our bookcase looking for something to read. Of all things, I found my hand resting on the old, black King James Bible. I settled back in my television chair and began to read starting on page one. It was boring. I decided to cheat a little and read the last chapter. I wanted to find out exactly what the preacher was talking about and what heaven was like. That one evening ruined my entire week. I did not get any rest or sleep for the next six nights. I read the book of Revelation every night and sometimes twice in one night. By the end of the week, I knew for sure I was hell bound.

By Friday night, I was exhausted. I went to bed but I kept thinking about all the sin in my life, and how I was destined for hell. I knew that I did not want to go to hell. Unfortunately, I did not know what to do. I did not know if God would, or even could forgive me. My life was so full of sin that I was powerless to know how to change. I wondered if God would ever forgive me! As I laid there in my bed, tears began to run down my cheeks. I did not know if I could do anything to reverse my life and get free from my sin. I was weary with my groaning; all night I wept, making my bed wet and drenching my pillow with tears (Psalms 6:6).

The next morning my pillow was soaked from the tears that streamed down my face all night long. At 8 am on Saturday, February 10, 1979, I became **"Radically-Saved."** I stood gazing out my bathroom window at two trees that were full of loud screeching birds. Suddenly, every bird stopped screeching. At that moment, I heard the audible voice of God say, **"I love you, you are Mine, you are forgiven."** I fell face down on the floor. It felt as if my skin was coming off my bones as I laid there. I was shaking all over and my tongue was going five miles a minute asking Jesus to forgive me of my sins and to save me. "<u>I love you, you are Mine, you are forgiven</u>" Those nine words changed the course of my life forever. I am so grateful that God took the time to speak those words to me that Saturday morning! Five years later, I realized that God had called me into the ministry (Matthew 22:14).

"But ye are a chosen generation, a royal priesthood, an holy nation, a peculiar people; that ye should shew forth the praises of him who hath called you out of darkness into his marvellous light. Which in time past were not a people, but are now the people of God, which had not obtained mercy, but now have obtained mercy" (1 Peter 2:9-10).

The moment I stood up I saw a bright, white light flash all the way down and through my entire body (Isaiah 1:18; 2 Corinthians 4:6). For the first time in my life, I actually felt clean inside. Something had "left" me, and the light, which had come in to me, was Jesus. Jesus is the light of the world (John 9:5). I agreed with Him and His word, He took my scarlet sins, and made them as white as snow. My sins were red like crimson, but He made them as white as wool (Isaiah 1:18). Jokingly, I began to tell everyone that I had received a spiritual Roto Rooter job from God. All joking aside, I was different, I felt different; I behaved different and for the first time in my life, I had a joyful feeling that I had never experienced before. I am so grateful that God is not a respecter of persons He accepts whoever fears Him and works righteousness (Acts 10:34-35).

I sat down in my favorite chair with that old, black King James Bible and began reading the New Testament. I was shocked and very amazed as I read. I began to feel something like electricity shooting from one side of my brain to the other side. For nearly a year every day as I read the word of God, I would feel the supernatural manifestation of electricity flowing through my brain. At times, I would spend six to eight hours just reading and praying the word of God into my life.

I soon learned that angels could appear in our dreams as someone we personally know. The very first week as a Christian I dreamed about a preacher I knew. In the dream, he said, "Get up and preach." The next thing I knew, I was preaching to a group of 500 young people. As I was waking, I heard the audible voice of God say "At the beginning of your supplications the command went out, and I have come to tell you, for you are greatly beloved; therefore consider the matter, and understand the vision" (Daniel 9:23).

I looked over at the clock next to my bed and it was flashing 3:33 am. Why it was flashing, I did not know. I got up and went into the kitchen. To my surprise, I found a book named Daniel in the Bible! I knew it was going to be a long night, so I turned on the coffee pot and spent the next four hours reading and praying over the book of Daniel (Jeremiah 33:3). By the time the sun was rising, I felt as if someone had plugged a 110 volt wire into my brain. It was buzzing with a hundred and one ideas and spiritual thoughts that were new and exciting to me.

During those first months of walking with the Lord, whenever I slept I would dream about whatever I had read in the scriptures earlier that day. It was as if I was reading scripture in my sleep. I had not read twenty five books in my entire lifetime; now I was reading the Bible relentlessly every day for hours at a time. I carried my Bible everywhere I went. I read it while I waited for my order at the local restaurant or as I sat in line at a fast food drive in. The word of God became my obsession because it cleansed me from all the attacks that came against my mind (Romans 12:1, 2).

The next day I went to the same church that my daughters attended. I walked the isle and made a public confession of faith in Jesus Christ asking Him into my heart again (Matthew 10:32). The pastor who was fresh out of seminary kept saying to me, "Now Brother Young, you have to repeat this sinner's prayer exactly like I am saying it or you won't go to heaven." I was glad to say any prayer and did not mind repeating the one he said. The moment I finished saying that prayer everyone in the church came up and congratulated me. As I stood at the front of the church shaking hands, and receiving words of encouragement from many of its members, an old white haired man shoved a clipboard in front of me and insisted that I fill out the paperwork before leaving. He said, "This way your name is on the roll." With my limited knowledge and understanding, I thought this was for the Book of Life. God possibly laughed more at the things I said and thought, than He had since the beginning of time (Luke 18:17).

As I moved out to the aisle to leave the building, two men approached me at the same time. I had never met either of them prior to that day. I listened to the two of them talk before we left the foyer, and it was evident they did not know each other. They spoke quietly between themselves and then asked if they could pray for me. I agreed and was ushered into a side room and asked to sit on a stool. As I sat there, they poured oil over my head and prayed in other tongues for one or two minutes each, and took turns prophesying over me. They stopped talking, smiled, said thank you, closed their Bibles, and headed for the door. Before leaving, one man identified himself as a prophet from a "Foursquare Church" in Northern California, and the other identified himself as a prophet from the "Church of God" out of Florida. They both told me the same story. According to them, the Holy Spirit had separately instructed them the month prior to come to this church to anoint the man who came forward for salvation that Sunday morning into the fivefold prophetic office. At the time, I did not know what that meant so I just smiled and said thank you and left. To this day, over thirty three years later, I have never seen either of these Prophets again. I do not even remember their names. I have often wondered if these two strangers could have been angels. They may have been ministering spirits sent forth to minister to me. We are to entertain strangers, for by so doing some may have, entertained angels (Hebrews 1:14; 13:2).

I was so excited about accepting Jesus Christ as my Savior, I felt as if I was walking on cloud nine. As soon as I arrived home, I called my mother, who lived five miles across town. I told her about the morning and that I had accepted Jesus Christ as my Savior. When I told her the name of the Church, she responded in an angry voice, "You know we are Assemblies of God!" The next thing I heard was the dial tone on the phone as my mother hung up on me. She was so upset with me for attending another denomination that she did not talk to me for nearly a year. I am still amazed today that some people are more concerned about what denomination you join, than the fact that you received salvation!

As I was pondering what had occurred with my mother the phone rang. The voice on the other end of the phone said, "Where is that plumber that was supposed to be at my house at 10 am this morning?" I immediately realized I had forgotten about the appointment. Normally, I would have responded to a question like that with a very plausible excuse. As I opened my mouth to respond to the question, I realized that God had done something special in me. In the past, I would have lied and not even thought about it. However, today was different; I did not have to lie. I felt a freedom down in my body I had never felt before. I felt free to tell the truth. For the first time in my entire life, I really felt free! Although I did not know exactly how it happened or where it came from, I enjoyed this new level of freedom. I had found truth and life and became free for the first time in my life (John 14:6: 8:32).

I apologized to the woman and told her I would reschedule her call for the first thing Monday morning, without feeling as if I needed to make any excuse. God had delivered and set me free from a lifetime of living with a lying spirit. It was gone forever. Thank God!

As I thought about everything that had happened, I heard a voice inside of my mind tell me to read John chapter fourteen. "I will pray the Father, and He will give you another Helper that He may abide with you forever the Spirit of truth" (John 14:17).

As I thought on those verses, it was as if a giant light bulb went off in my mind. The reason I was able to tell the truth was because Jesus had set me free from an earthly spirit! Everyone is born with a natural inclination to lie. My parents never had to teach me to lie it came naturally. We are all the children of our father, the devil, who is the father of lies, until we are born again and set free from his lying spirit. We all belong to the devil until we willfully chose to accept the work Christ Jesus did on our behalf at Calvary. The devil was a murderer from the beginning and has no truth in him. When he speaks a lie, he speaks from his own resources, for he is a liar and the father of it (John 8:44).

That following week I made a special point to go visit my pastor about the two men who prayed for me, anointed me with oil and prophesied over me. The pastor spent no time even considering the idea that the two men had been sent by God. Instead, he kept trying to convince me to forget it all. He explained that for the last two thousand years there was no longer any need for the offices of the Apostles or Prophets. He told me that the 20th century Apostle and Prophet was just a regular old preacher with a fancier title.

As I left his office, I wondered why he began sweating profusely while he tried to explain that I was thinking incorrectly. I began to think that he was perhaps the one who was thinking incorrectly. My concerns had now become his concerns. I had not been home five minutes before my pastor called. He did not wait to preempt his call with a pleasant greeting, but began rattling off scriptures to prove that the pastoral office was the only office God recognized. Thank God, he was wrong! I realized there is only one listing for the office of a pastor, which is in (Jeremiah 17:16). "As for me, I have not hurried away from being a shepherd (a pastor), who follows you..."

A Mental Renewing

In the months following my salvation, I told everyone I met what Jesus Christ had done for me, and what He wanted to do for them. "The Romans Road" gospel track was a divine gift from God. I had been studying the book of Romans for several weeks when verses one and two of chapter 12 jumped off the page and into my heart. When the Holy Spirit said, "Because you are refusing to be conformed to this world your mind is being renewed and transformed by the living word of your creator which will allow you to prove what is that good, and acceptable, and perfect, will that He has for your life."

I had made a choice to abandon all of my personal desires and hobbies (hunting, fishing, camping, television etc...) in exchange for building a deeper relationship with Jesus. Because of that personal commitment, I moved forward in leaps and bounds as I daily communed with the Lord. I was constantly bathing and washing myself with the living life changing water of His word (John 15:3).

I was accustomed to the electricity shooting from one side of my brain to the other and I do not know the exact time I realized it was no longer present as I read the Bible. On that day, I fell to my knees and began to repent. After a minute or so I thought, "What am I repenting for?" I was not in sin and not having the electricity was not a sin. As I stood, I sensed in my spirit all was well and everything was ok. Several months later, I realized I had received a healing in my mind. To this very day, I often long for those early days of the electrifying sensation that gave a personal feeling of God and His word.

The following weeks, as I thought about the absence of the electricity in my mind while reading the Bible I joyfully began to realize that God had healed my learning disability. The first year of my salvation I read my Bible four to six hours each day. Since my salvation, I have read thousands of books including my Bible on a consistent basis and I am able to retain a great deal of what I read. I have not attempted to memorize statements or scripture but somehow I do. I do not remember everything I have read, but usually enough to find it quickly.

Exodus 3:2

During the second year as a Christian I had read about God speaking to Moses at the burning bush. While driving on the way to a job, I wondered what Moses thought when he saw the burning bush.

Glancing at my watch, I remembered I was early for my appointment so, I parked at a rest stop and reread the story of Moses at the burning bush. As I was reading, I became aware that a small tree fifty feet in front of me was on fire. I saw no one around and began to ask myself "how the fire began." While I sat there, I heard the Holy Spirit say, "That was the first thing Moses asked also." I began to wonder how I could get God to notice me when I heard the Holy Spirit say, "God saw your heart turn aside this morning as you prayed." When I heard that, an inward peace over took me like a warm breeze.

As I watched the tree burn, I then began to hope that God would audibly speak to me as He did Moses. To my dismay, the fire dwindled out and I did not hear the audible voice of God that day. However, I did hear the Holy Spirit. Often I ponder my life and many times my thoughts return to that day and the small tree that was on fire. When the fire was totally out it did not look like the tree that had been on fire at all. The leaves were still green and the bark was not burned or scorched.

Years later I had a minister tell me that God just wanted me to know that He is not a respecter of persons. What He has done in the lives of others He will also do for me because He loves to see my reaction to the teachings of His word. Matthew 7 tells us to "Ask, Seek, and Knock." Keep on asking!

If we never ask, we will never receive, if we never seek, we will never locate the blessings of God, and if we never knock on the door, it will remain closed. We must (**A.S.K.**).

The Prayer Closet

As a baby Christian, I took the Word of God literally. While attending a tent meeting the speaker said, "Gods power comes with a price" and I was determined to pay any price required. Previously, I had heard several radio preachers say; "Go into your closet and when you have shut the door, you will find God and you may recover whatever you have lost due to slothfulness." I was determined to regain anything I had lost. My secret place of prayer became my bedroom closet. I would go in and shut the door knowing that if my Father saw me in secret, He would reward me openly (Matthew 6:6).

A sure cure for the lukewarm, slothful Laodicean spirit is hungering and thirsting for righteousness. If we abstain from food, we will surely hunger, and if we abstain from water, we will surely thirst. This is what I call a total fast. I realized if I fasted and delighted myself in God and His righteousness, He would fill me with His desires for my life (Matthew 5:6: 6:16).

Many of the saints fasted three days and nights without food or water and that was what I chose to do. I do not recommend anyone doing this. It is difficult beyond human imagination. I have learned over the years to seek God on how long to fast. I no longer just chose a number of days and fast that length of time.

Queen Esther called for a three day total fast which spared the Jews from total annihilation (Esther 4:16). The King of Nineveh called for a total fast and God relented from destroying the people of Nineveh (Jonah 3:7). The Apostle Paul forcibly entered into a (no food or water) total fast (Acts 9:9).

During those early years, I did foolish things because I was hungry for the things of God. I am a little over six feet tall, but that did not stop me from going into my four by six–foot clothes closet and spending hours at a time on my knees in prayer; with dress clothes hanging on one side and work clothes hanging on the other. I was not sure what the verse meant about praying in secret; for some reason I had the impression that meant to be in the dark so others cannot see you. Therefore, I did not turn on the light.

All of this made my prayer closet even more interesting. Once I was kneeling in total darkness and somehow I became tangled up with a belt that was hanging from a shelf. I must have pulled on the belt because the next thing I knew I had four or five boxes falling down upon my head!

Since I was self-employed, I had a lot of free time, which I used in prayer and Bible reading. Most of the time I would go into my clothes closet and pray; I never considered the cleanness of the work clothes I was wearing. One day my oldest daughter, as she putting away my clean clothes, said, "Dad, all of your clothes stink; have you been hanging your dirty clothes up with the clean clothes?" That was the day I found myself a different prayer closet.

When I thought of using my wife's "walk in closet," it was as if a light bulb had gone off in my mind. Her closet was three times larger than mine. I wondered why I did not think of that in the first place. It never entered my mind to discuss this with her. I just carried on with my new idea. The next day, I went into her closet shut the door, got down on my knees, and began to pray, while thinking, "Man! It is sure roomy in here." When I am by myself in prayer, I often pray aloud. I had been praying for about an hour when the door suddenly opened. My wife was holding an arm full of folded clothes. Surprised to find someone in her closet, she screamed as the clothes went flying in every direction. My first thought was, she should have knocked. She said, "What are you doing in my closet?" I was a little startled myself and very disappointed. This was the second time in just one week that I had to find myself a different prayer closet (Luke 18:17)!

My new prayer closet became the front seat of my work van. Although it did not allow me to be in the dark nor on, my knees when praying it certainly served the purpose! I soon found myself parked on the bay front watching the big ocean liners and fishing vessels pass back and forth. During those early days, I wept much for Gods perfect will for my loved ones and for His church (Romans 12:2).

I was always trying to find a better and more secluded location to pray, but just could not locate one. The day came when I laid all my prayer closet desires down. I heard the Holy Spirit say to me, "Great spot. You are called to be a fisher of souls." I wept tears at God's words to me and began to pray with a greater joy over the souls who need to come into the Kingdom of God.

Hearing God at Unexpected Times

I began to hear God speak to me at odd times, especially when I was not in prayer. The Lord spoke to me once while taking a bath. When this happened, I almost jumped out of my skin. I said, "Lord I am not dressed." I look back and realize God must have had a good laugh at that one.

Romans 10:15 says, "How beautiful are the feet of those that preach the gospel of peace, and bring glad tidings of good things." After reading that verse, I began to notice how dry and ugly my feet were. I definitely wanted to preach the gospel and wondered if God considered my feet less then beautiful. That night I began a rigorous routine of washing, massaging and applying lotion to my feet. After several weeks, I realized it was a waste of time and my feet were no better looking. I remembered the stuff my wife used on her feet a product called "Pretty Feet." I began using Pretty Feet every morning and night. Although my feet never looked any better, my hands became much softer so I discontinued using the product.

I continued praying about the situation concerning my feet until the Holy Spirit gave me a revelation. He revealed that I had totally misunderstood the verse. In a vision, I saw a man walk into a room and share the gospel with everyone present. Everyone was glad he came. To them, he spiritually had beautiful feet because it was his feet that carried him to them to share "The Good News Gospel!" Thank God, now I could stop worrying that my feet would disqualify me. I then knew God considered my feet beautiful whenever I shared "The Good News Gospel!"

One evening as I was thinking about all my attempts to make my feet beautiful, the Holy Spirit explained to me why Jesus washed the feet of His disciples in John chapter thirteen saying "When we pray for another person to walk in the blessing of God that is spiritually washing their feet." Jesus washed His disciple's feet in the natural. We are washing the feet of others in the spiritual realm when we pray for them (John 13:10; 15:3; 1 Corinthians 15:46).

SECTION #2
1980

Forgiveness at Work

I heard a sermon on forgiving the debts of others. The crux of the message was, "If I did not forgive the debt of others, God would not forgive my debts" (Matthew 6:12). These debts could be in the natural or in the spiritual (1Corinthians 15:46). During the next two weeks, I prayed and studied everything I could find on the pastors text.

By the end of the second week, conviction came and I knew I needed to forgive not only the spiritual debts I was due by others, but also the financial debts many owed me. I went into my office and pulled out a file that contained a list of homeowners who owed my company money for over two years. The sum totaled over $18,000. Many of those who owed me lived in low–income houses, and had fallen on hard times because of the poor economy.

I sat down and wrote a letter that went something like this: "I am a Christian who practices what I preach. The Bible says that we are to forgive our debtors. Evidently, you must have fallen on some hard times otherwise you would have paid off your debt you owe my company. Therefore, in the name of Jesus Christ, I choose to forgive all that you owe my company for any work performed on your property. May the Lord Jesus Christ bless you, and keep you and your loved ones safe."

With a single, stoke of my pen I forgave 200 families over $18,000. When my accountant heard what I had done, he asked, "Are you crazy?" Because of that action, I paid no taxes for two years. My corporate attorney listed my company in a class action suit and I received a $44,000 settlement. That same year I sold my business for a high five–digit figure.

I learned firsthand that every good and every perfect gift is from above, and comes down from the Father of lights, with whom is no variableness, neither shadow of turning (James 1:17).

I had given, or in my case, I had forgiven and had become financially blessed. I received back in good measure, pressed down, and shaken together, and running over, men gave to me. The same measure that I used was the measurement used for me in return (Luke 6:38).

Supernatural Help

My second year as a radical believer my pastor informed the church I was to preach at the Wednesday night service in three weeks. Although the pastor knew I had never preached in my life, he specifically asked if I would deliver the message. The church had five deacons and any one of them could have filled the pulpit in the pastor's absence. During the next two weeks I prayed, fasted, and prepared my sermon. My text:

"Whosoever therefore shall confess me before men, him will I confess also before my Father which is in heaven. But whosoever shall deny me before men, him will I also deny before my Father which is in heaven" (Matthew 10: 32-33).

 I was surprised when I agreed because I did not know where the "Yes" had come from when I was asked to preach. I was going to say "No" or "I am not sure," but when I opened my mouth, I heard the words "Yes I will do it." Driving home, I kept wondering where those five words came from. The one thing that amazed me was the words were not from my mind. They came up out of my belly from out of my spirit. The words were like a flowing river of living water (John 7:38).
 I never realized that preaching was such a costly profession. Immediately after the pastor informed everyone that I was going to preach in his absence, two deacons approached me and asked, "Do you own a suit brother Young?" I didn't! A plumber does not have a need to own a dress suit. The deacons let me know I needed a suit, so the following day I purchased my first three piece polyester, brown pin striped suit. I wore it only once: the day I preached.
 Wednesday night arrived too soon for me. Although I had prepared for over three weeks, I still had an uneasy feeling attacking my thoughts. I was fearful of forgetting my message. In high school when I stood up to speak, a spirit of the fear came upon me so badly that I shook and

stuttered and no one could understand what I said. That evening when I stepped behind the pulpit, none of my preparation came to my mind. Fear once again swept through me. I began to tremble so badly that the pulpit began to make a knocking sound on the wooden floor. I opened my mouth to give the opening prayer and all that came out was stuttering mixed with my trembling voice. Under my breath, I said, "Lord Jesus, if you do not help me I will walk out that door and never come back."

Jesus came to my aid and helped me, but it was not because of my demand, it was because of His "Loving Grace." The Lord Jesus wanted to reveal Himself to me. He is the only one who has authority and power over "ALL" human conditions and circumstances.

The noise of the pulpit rattling on the floor and my trembling voice became so disturbing to me, I was about to close my Bible and walk out the door when the air around the pulpit where I was standing felt electrified. I then heard an audible voice on my right side and behind me. I turned to look but saw no one. I thought the other people in the congregation could hear also the voice, but it became quite evident that they could not. The voice said, "Peace Be Still" and I suddenly, "felt" peace. I repeated exactly what I had heard to the congregation "Peace Be Still."

For the next thirty-five minutes, the audible voice used the exact same text that I had chosen for my sermon. All I did was repeat whatever I heard, "Word for word." I felt the presence of a supernatural being and heard an audible voice the entire time. I had only been speaking about ten minutes, when some of the people began to cry and confess their sin aloud publicly as they came down to the prayer altar. Some fell on their face at the prayer altar and began to pray aloud. I did not know what was happening. These people were crying out while confessing sins of adultery and fornication. Their cries become so loud I had to quit preaching three times for over a minute and just stand there in wonder. When I finished preaching, only one man remained sitting in a pew. Everyone else was on their knees repenting of their sins. The prayer altar had no room for anyone else. People were lying in the aisles sobbing and trembling. At this point, I realized I no longer felt electrified and the angel of the Lord was gone. I carefully made my way off the platform and went to the back of the building as people began to dry their eyes and leave the building.

That was my first experience with preaching. I am so grateful that God showed up and showed out! I repented for having a bad attitude in the beginning when I wanted to leave the church and not come back. Several years later, an old prophet told me that the first time I preached was a foretaste of how I would minister during the end times. I often pray for God to hurry up and get "The End Times" here. I really enjoy the prophetic preaching, and teaching. God is so good; He is a stronghold in the day of trouble; and He knows those who trust in Him (Nahum 1:7).

To my dismay that was the one and only time, the angel of the Lord showed up to aid in my preaching. Although, I have the assurance that one day this will be the norm when I speak or step behind a podium–that period has not yet begun.

Drawing Closer

I want to say that I am the least deserving of all saints, who has received Gods gifts and anointing. In addition, these manifested blessings and endless treasures that are in Christ Jesus did not appear over night. In fact, it has taken me over 33 years to grasp what small measure of the anointing I have (Ephesians 3:8)!

It was exciting when I found out I could be as close to God as I wanted to be. I found myself on my knees every opportunity, seeking His face to know His will for my life. I did not have any particular game plan in my attempt to get closer to God; I just did my best to find Him every chance I had. I submitted myself to God and resisted the devil as I drew near to God. Each day I cleansed my hands in repentance and purified my heart as I resisted all temptations of double-mindedness (James 4:7-8).

Unfortunately, many miss the first part of these scriptures. We are to submit to God. Resist the devil. Only then, can we draw near to God in full assurance that He will draw near to us. I soon realized the more time I spent reading the Bible, praying and waiting before God the more sensitive I became to the situations around me and in the lives of other people. I had personally tasted the living word of God (Psalms 34:8). I knew that the Lord is good and a strong hold in the day of trouble the Lord blesses the individual who trusts in Him (Nahum 1:7).

In a dream I was shown a major sin Christians deal with is double-mindedness. Many waver from having God-like faith to no faith at all. One day they have hope and the next day no hope. Many have based their love on feelings instead of His word. Therefore, what little love they have often dwindles to nothing. This is double-mindedness. All forms of double-mindedness come to steal, kill, and destroy our blessings.

I was hungry to hear His living prophetic voice on a daily basis. I wanted the manifested presence of the Lord Jesus Christ to invade my entire spirit, soul and body. For two years, every morning and evening, seven days a week three hundred sixty five days a year, I would stand before a mirror, look at myself, and point at myself with my index finger and say, "Duane, God is not a respecter of persons, what He has done for others God will do for you" (Galatians 2:6). "Duane, God is not a man and He does not lie. What He has said, He will do (Numbers 23:19). He has promised that His word shall not return void, but it shall accomplish that which He pleases, and it shall prosper in the thing where He sends it" (Isaiah 55:11).

During those days, I prophesied thousands of scriptures over myself right out of my Bible. During the past thirty-three years, I have seen many of those prophetic words come to pass in my life. It was during those early years that I had an insatiable hunger for the prophetic word of God to invade my everyday life. I did not just want His word, will and way on Sunday and Wednesday, I wanted it every day and if possible, every hour. I ate, drank, and slept His living word (Jeremiah 15:16).

I attended every prophetic meeting within a hundred mile radius of my hometown. It did not matter if it was a man or woman speaking. I submitted myself to the prophetic anointing to lay hold of a supernatural walk with God. Every opportunity I had to have hands laid on me for an impartation of a similar gifting as the speaker I jumped at. No one ever refused to pray for me. At times when they laid hands on me, I would feel fire fall from the throne of God and flow through me. At other times, I felt nothing but in faith I said, "Yes Lord God I receive a like anointing as this man or woman."

Because of the great lack of one on one, prophetic teaching and mentoring in the body of Christ, I am writing a book called <u>The Seven Realms of the Prophetic</u>." In its teaching, I explain how each realm of the prophetic is clearly distinct from the others with understanding that could possibly change a person's entire walk with God. I had come to the revelation of verbalizing the word of God over my life and I teach others how to do the same.

An angel appeared in a dream and told me to confess the word of God over my life as well as all the supernatural things that I wanted in my life. In the dream, I saw an angel standing over me declaring that I was not to live by bread alone, but by every word of God (Luke 4:4). When I awoke I determined I was not going to live by bread alone, but by the living word of God, which is the spiritual manna from heaven the fresh hot living bread of life. Spiritual manna is not old, cold, moldy, dried out, hard, and stale. The bread from heaven is without leaven. For a season, the Lord had humbled me and allowed me to hunger spiritually for His word. He then fed me with manna the living bread from heaven fresh Rhema. I did not know of this Rhema nor did my father know of it. This Rhema only proceeds from the mouth of the Lord (Deuteronomy 8:3).

To my knowledge, during those early years in South Texas, no one was walking in the office of a prophet, but that did not stop me from searching it out. It is the glory of God to conceal a thing: but the honor of a king is to search out the word of God (Proverbs 25:2).

I have learned God hides or conceals a thing from us to see just how hungry we are for it. Eventually, I had acquired someone's prophetic mailing list. I sent out post cards and called everyone the Holy Spirit pointed out. Within a few weeks, I had a dozen newsletters that listed future meetings. Some of these prophetic gatherings were good and some of them were very, very questionable. Because of this, I have personally adopted a saying by Rick Joyner and trained myself to do likewise…"Swallow the meat and spit out the bones."

When I began prophesying over myself, I did not really know what I was doing. It was like shooting in the dark. I did however believe the word of God concerning the confession of our words. I just did not fully realize the impact that our words would have on us. Daily we eat the words that we had previously spoken. It does not matter if the words were positive or negative; they were all prophetic in the sight of God. We have the power to speak living words or words of death. My belly shall be satisfied with the fruit of my mouth and with the increase of my lips shall I be filled. Death and life are in the power of my tongue: and I shall eat the fruit of the words that I speak (Proverbs 18:20-21).

I did not have a complete understanding but I have learned if you say it, you have prayed it. "Oh, God let the words of my mouth, and the meditation of my heart, be acceptable in thy sight, my strength, and my redeemer." God heard my prayer and gave ear to the words of my mouth (Psalms 19:14; 54:2).

Every time a prophet came within one hundred miles of my hometown, I would go and sit under that anointing. I knew that if you hung around someone with the flu you would soon catch the flu. Therefore, when I came to the understanding that this same principle works with the gifts and anointing of God, I took every opportunity to seek out these prophetic men and women of God. Yes, that is not a typo. I did say prophetic women of God. I wanted the prophet's reward; it did not matter to me whether or not it came from a male or a female. As my wife says, according to Biblical definition, a woman is a man with a womb. Scriptures that refer to "men" are also for women to obey. He who receives a prophet in the name of a prophet shall receive a prophet's reward (Matthew 10:41). The prophet's reward is God, supplying all of our needs according to his riches in glory by Christ Jesus (Philippians 4:19).

I once left my house at daylight and drove four hours to a very special prophetic meeting. When I arrived people had already began to form a line. I stood in line with five hundred other people for six hours just to ensure I could get a decent seat. The doors opened at 7 pm and I was blessed to get a seat within viewing distance of the platform and I did not have to watch the meeting on the overhead monitor, as many others did.

The meeting ended after 11 p.m. and I still had a four hour drive back home. I was a little saddened with the meeting. I had felt sure it would have been an awesome gathering. As I drove home and pondered all I had heard and had seen that night, the Holy Spirit impressed upon me that my efforts of sacrifice were acceptable in the sight of God the Father. God looks on the heart and its motives. I had paid a price to lay hold of the blessing of God and He made sure I knew my sacrifice of love would not go without a reward.

Several months later, the Holy Spirit gave me a complete understanding of what I had been exposed to that evening. The word had to ferment within my spirit man before it solidified and became Rhema. I was often surprised as I would be sharing the gospel with one of my customers and in my mind, the words I was saying sounded to me as if they were the same words coming from the prophetic meeting I had attended months earlier. That was and still is one of my many rewards, which is a mighty blessing.

God honors every free will offering and sacrifice I give to Him. The greater my sacrifice or offering, the greater my reward will be. Whenever I want something I have never had, I will always have to do something I have never done. I will only possess what I passionately pursue.

"Filled - Healed - Delivered"

One Sunday during a Bible study, my stomach became extremely nauseated to the point of vomiting. The pastor heard that I had become physically ill; and asked if I would come forward to receive prayer. He did not have to ask a second time. The words were still in the airways, and I was down front with both hands lifted up. He prayed, as usual, and I did not really feel any special touch at that time.

I returned to my seat and it was like a time-delayed bomb when it happened. I began giggling and felt drunk. Now, I knew what it felt like to be drunk, but I had never experienced anything like this. I was about to experience a divine supernatural healing like nothing I had ever heard of before. Looking back, I now realize things I did earlier in the week had prepared the way for this encounter.

The previous Sunday morning, I had given an extra offering. It was not that much, just a little something over and above my tithe. I had also been doing a little fasting. Because I did hard physical work, I could not stop eating all together, so I chose to eat only once a day. During this same time, I spent a little extra time in prayer, Bible reading and waiting on God. Without realizing it, I had aligned myself with what I call "A Threefold Cord of Grace." When you give, when you pray, and when you fast. Notice the Bible does not say, "If you give, pray or fast; but when you do those things."

"But when you do a charitable deed of giving, do not let your left hand know what your right hand is doing, that your charitable deed may be in secret; and your Father who sees in secret will Himself reward you openly. However, you, when you pray, go into your room, and when you have shut your door, pray to your Father who is in the secret place; and your Father who sees in secret will reward you openly. But you, when you fast, anoint your head and wash your face, so that you do not appear to men to be fasting, but to your Father who is in the secret place; and your Father who sees in secret will reward you openly" (Matthew 6:3-4, 6, 17-18).

During that Sunday evening Bible study meeting, God chose to touch me and miraculously heal me from two existing lung conditions. Emphysema (excessive swelling of tissue in my lungs) and Pleurisy with the slang name "Devils grip" which makes breathing excruciating painful. I had caused both conditions to come upon me because I began smoking non–filtered cigarettes at the age of ten and by the time I was thirty I was addicted to nicotine and smoking three packs of extra super long cigarettes a day. When I did not have a cigarette in my mouth, it was full of chewing tobacco or snuff I would sometimes wake up to smoke a cigarette in the middle of the night.

The Lord God healed me of both Emphysema and Pleurisy that Sunday night. Although my lungs ached with excruciating pain, and at times I could barely breathe, I made sure I never missed a church service. The evening the pastor prayed for me, I became drunk with the "New Wine" from the spirit of God. The gospel of Mark speaks about this new wine. I was "FILLED" with this New Wine, which is also called the unmerited grace and favor of God. No one puts New Wine into old wineskins; or else the new wine bursts the wineskins and the New Wine and the wineskins are ruined. However, we do put New Wine into new wineskins (Mark 2:22).

King Solomon revealed a direct connection between the receiving of the New Wine and sacrificial obedience unto God. When we honor God with everything we own by giving him the first and the best, our barns will burst and our wine vats (container) will brim over and overflow with New Wine (Proverbs 3:9-10). The New Testament believer is the container, which operates in both the natural and spiritual realms. The Lord will pour out upon such zealous believers both a natural blessing and an increase of the Holy Spirits spiritual blessings.

Without realizing it, I had prepared this old wine skin to receive the New Wine for my time. The New Wine is different for ever season of life. Everyone is responsible for preparing his or her own wine skin to accommodate the New Wine for his time. The time and care that we give to the preparation (bible study, prayer, fasting, giving of our time, treasure or talents etc...) of our wine skin will determine the level, power, and authority of the New Wine that we will receive. To everything, there is a season, and a time to every purpose under the heaven (Ecclesiastes 3:1).

During the past thirty years, the church has experienced small splashes of the New Wine. This was only a foretaste of the early and latter rains coming together (Deuteronomy 11:14; James 5:7).

Jesus referred to the New Wine as the best wine in the gospel of John. Jesus even gives us its secret recipe. All we need to do is follow what He said in order to make our own "New wine," which was also referred to as "The Best Wine" (John 2:10). We are the earthen vessels. We are the water pots and when we are full of the living water (the word of God) which flows from the river of life and only when we are totally full of living water will it turn into the New Wine and not one second or ounce prior. We may then draw out the New Wine and serve it to our guest. This is "The Best Wine the New Wine" that God has been patiently holding back and waiting to pour it out on us during the last days (John 2:6-10).

The Lord has given me an entire teaching on "The wedding in Cana of Galilee," but for now I will only address a small portion of this passage. The number 'Six,' always refers to man. On the sixth day of creation, God created man. Water often speaks of the living word, will and way of God. The water of the word of God spiritually washes the believer as they read scripture. The more we read and apply the Bible to our life, the cleaner we become (John 4:10; 15:3).

The very first thing an individual has to do, is to be filled up to the brim, and running over with the living water of God. That is when the Lord speaks to the water and it becomes "The New Wine" or the best wine. Every season and period in history has had its own New Wine or "The Best Wine" for that time. Every season was and is different. The New Wine is to meet the needs of the people who are drawing near to God during that particular season. The New Wine God pours out on one person could be very different from the New Wine He pours out on someone else. Many times, I will pray, "Lord God I want my water turned into the new wine. I want the New Wine without measure. It does not matter what flavor, fragrance or color the New Wine is. I do however want it in full strength make it extra strong."

Although I was drunk in the spirit, I finally managed to make it to my work van after the Sunday service. I was a radical believer; however, I was still a very religious man. I "Did Not" carry cigarettes into the church. As I was pulling out of the parking lot, I lit up a cigarette and with one breath I realized my lungs did not hurt. I remember waving my hand out the window as I said, "Thank you Jesus. I am "HEALED." God reversed the curse. Thank you Lord Jesus. The goodness of the Lord passed before me He was gracious to me therefore I will declare the name of the Lord God forever (Exodus 33:19). He has mercy on whomever He chooses and compassion on whomever He chooses (Romans 9:15).

God had healed me. I had received a miracle. I had no pain at all in breathing or inhaling cigarettes, which now I see was a stupid thing to keep doing. There were days following my healing when I wondered if that horrible pain would return, I would proclaim, "No, I am healed. I am healed forever more!" I hated smoking or smelling like smoke, but I was addicted. I began to wonder why God healed me first before delivering me from this nasty habit. That one question kept coming to mind. Eventually that question bothered me so greatly that I had to ask the Lord to remove that one question from my mind. I had decided that God had left me to deal with it myself. I continued to try different things to get free from the cigarettes. I eventually cut back some, although I knew I was still hooked on nicotine.

An Appointed Day of Deliverance

The day Jesus set me free from smoking over three packs of extra long cigarettes a day, was definitely one of the greatest days of my entire life. The only way I could have smoked more cigarettes was to get up earlier in the morning. God's miraculous touch happened on a Thursday evening during a home group meeting in 1984, five years after I heard the audible voice of God. My Christian faith and life was a radical life of dynamic faith. I shared Jesus everywhere I went and with everyone I saw.

The entire time, I had been learning things from the Bible that did not make much sense to me until "after the fact." On three different occasions, the same prophetic word over me was that God was teaching me about numerology (I have written a book on numerology). At that time, I did not really know anything about numerology, nor did I fully understand the interpretation of the prophetic words.

I had tried to quit smoking a number of times with no success. One day I woke up with an idea. I did not start smoking three packs of cigarettes a day; I began by smoking a few cigarettes a day. Before I realized it, I was hooked and smoking sixty cigarettes a day. I decided that I would cut my cigarette intake down a little at a time. I planned to do this over a year if necessary.

The first two months I smoked fifty cigarettes a day. I had also managed to quit chewing the nicotine gum (in place of regular gum for enjoyment), dipping snuff and chewing tobacco, which also gave me hope that one day I would walk in total deliverance.

From the third to the fifth month, I went down to thirty cigarettes a day. By the end of the eight month, I was smoking only eight cigarettes a day.

I was miserable. The truth is I felt guilty because I enjoyed smoking cigarettes. I began to realize I needed God to do something more than just set me free from smoking. God needed to remove my addiction to nicotine if I was going to remain "Free" for the rest of my life. During this entire time, I smoked a pipe on weekends, but I had never considered it as a smoking habit.

During the fifth month, I began crying out to God to remember His covenant of circumcision He had with me. I began praying that prayer for several weeks, and then the urge to pray that particular prayer lifted as fast as the urge had come. At this particular time, I was unaware the number "five" represented Gods divine grace. During the fifth month, the grace and favor of God showed up in my life and kept me on target! The fifth time Noah's name is recorded in scripture he received grace from the Lord (Genesis 6:8). The fifth time we find the name of Ruth, the Moabitess, is when she receives grace—grace that came through Boaz from God (Ruth 2:2).

I was only smoking eight cigarettes a day when I reached the eight month of trying to quit. I was also unaware the number "eight" represented new beginnings. When I found out what the number eight represented, I began calling out to God for His divine favor and grace to over take me and deliver me.

God commanded that every male child be dedicated to Him on the eighth day through the act of circumcision. The very act of circumcision had become a ritual to the children of Israel instead of the intended relationship builder God intended (Genesis 17:12). Circumcision was to open the way for all of humanity to have a covenant relationship with a living God. Although it regressed into a legalistic ritual, God waited patiently while Noah built the Ark. The salvation of eight souls came through water, which is also a prophetic type salvation by circumcision (1 Peter 3:20). I felt God wanted to give me a new beginning similar to Noah.

Jesus appeared to all twelve disciples after eight days saying, "Peace to you" (John 20:26). Jesus wanted to reveal this same loving kindness to me in an extremely profound way. He did this by supernaturally delivering me from an addiction of nicotine, which is legal throughout the earth—more people are addicted to nicotine than to alcohol or even illegal drugs.

I give thanks to God the Father and the Lord Jesus Christ; I have not had a cigarette since that day. For over twenty–five years I have walked, free of cigarettes and the addiction of nicotine. Praise God! I was visiting, a home group when the leader announced, "Someone here has been doing all they can to stop smoking and be free of nicotine!" My friend who had brought me to the meeting nudged me and whispered, "That's you!" Then the speaker said, "The Lord says, He is going to set you free for the rest of your life if you will come forward now!" I jumped up and ran over to stand in front of the pastor. He reached out and touched my forehead with his index finger that he had anointed with oil, and said, "Be free, according to the word of the Lord!" It felt like a bolt of lightning hit me I went four feet backwards hit a wall and slid down on my butt. Because I believed the prophetic word spoken over me, I have walked free since that day (2 Chronicles 20:20c).

I have had many people ask me to pray for their deliverance from cigarettes. Unfortunately, the majority of these people are not serious nor have they actually attempted to quit. They are looking for an easy out. I hate to tell anyone this, but there is no easy out. When you get serious with God about quitting, He will deliver you. I have seen deliverance come to those who have their backs against the wall. Although they have tried and have failed, they have not quit trying. That is when God shows up and shows out. He gets all the glory.

A Changed Man

A week after my deliverance from nicotine, while working at a home, I felt the spirit of peace as I entered; I was in the home of a believer. As I worked, the woman began to share her faith in Christ. When I asked about her husband she said, "He could not hold a job, he was rude, crude, and obnoxious, and no one wanted to be around him." She went on to say that her friends waited until he left to play cards with others before coming over to visit.

To my disappointment, I ran out of material and would have to return later to complete her job. She told me that she would be gone, but her no account husband should be home when I returned.

I returned and completed the job and was leaving when her husband began to shout at me that I had disturbed his day. I was about to say something apologetic when the spirit of God rose up within me saying, "You have been called from birth to be a minister of the gospel of Jesus Christ. You have run long enough. You are to be a gatekeeper in the house of God says the Lord." He stood there with his mouth open in shock as I carried my tools to my van.

When I saw he had followed me to my van, I turned and looked him in the eyes and commanded all anger and bitterness to come out of him in Jesus' name.

Two months later, while working at that same house the woman said, "I do not know what you said to my husband but he is no longer the way he was before. He has been at the same job for two months and that is a record for him. He no longer drinks and plays cards." Standing to her feet, she pointed her index finger in my face and said, "In fact, he has even quit smoking, and he went to church with me that same night and has never missed a service since, "Praise you Lord Jesus."" In addition, he is the first one at church every time we meet.

This is the prophetic picture of what the power of God will do for all in need if they will hear the living word of God.

Free At Last

I had finished one job and was getting in my van when a young boy said; "my momma wants to know if you can fix her kitchen faucet." I picked up my toolbox and followed the boy into his house. The first thing I noticed was his mother lying on the couch doubled over and moaning in pain.

I paused and asked if I could pray for her? She nodded yes but then motioned for her son to go next door to get his brothers to agree with us in prayer. Within a few minutes, three men walked in the front door—all of them stood nearly seven feet tall. I had to look up to see their faces. For a few moments, I thought, "Oh God what did I get myself into?" Reaching over I laid my hands on the top of her head and canceled all assignments against her in Jesus' name. All of a sudden, the power of God came into the room and the woman jumped up from the couch and began to dance and shout in other tongues. She then began singing "I am free, I am free at last." One son told me that she had been bedridden for over six months.

Several months later as I was driving past her house, I saw her sitting on the front porch. I stopped to get a report; she told me she felt better ever since the day I prayed with her. Notice I prayed with her, NOT for her. The six of us had come into the power of agreement and she received her miracle (Matthew 18:19).

Marketing

As I sat praying and worshipping God His presence became so powerful I could barely stand. I glanced upwards to shout, I love You, when the heavens parted. With my naked eyes and ears, I could see and hear thousands of angels singing. As I stood there in total awe, I began to sing along with them while wondering how I knew these lyrics. The music and the songs were greater than anything I had ever heard in my life.

All of a sudden, my carnal mind began thinking if I had a tape recorder I could make a small fortune with these songs. With that very thought and at that exact moment, the heavens snapped shut like a curtain closing. Instantaneously everything disappeared from my sight and hearing.

I immediately fell to my knees repenting for wanting to market the things of God but that did not reopen the heavens. I had become an extremely sad individual. That may have been lesson number 150,000 that I had to learn the hard way (John 2:13-17).

Questions lead to Learning

During the first five years of my salvation, I became concerned about my dreams. Whatever I dreamed happened within several weeks. No matter what I dreamed, it occurred as I had seen in the dream. When I spoke to my pastor concerning my dreams and how they were happening he leaned back in his chair, looked up at the ceiling and said, "Brother Young you have been eating way too much pizza." His seminary explanations lasted about a week before I realized his answers were incorrect. He did not believe my dreams were from God. Therefore, I turned to my Bible and found the correct answers "The prophet that hath a dream let him tell a dream and he that has My word let him speak My word faithfully" (Jeremiah 23:28).

After I settled that question, my dreams seemed to increase in number. Not all of my dreams are prophetic, but, at that particular time in my life, the majority of my dreams were very prophetic because God was teaching me Himself. I have to admit, I did not always get the exact understanding or revelation each time. There are times when I miss it totally. Nevertheless, I have continually grown both from the correct interpretation and from the incorrect interpretation. I try to leave room for God to show up in any way He wants. I have learned there are three aspects to a dream from God.

First, we have the revelation or the dream itself. **Second**, we have the interpretation. What is God saying? **Lastly**, we have the application, which tells us how and what we will have to do to fulfill our part of the dream if we have any part in it at all.

It was during this same time I felt the leading of the Holy Spirit that I was to move to a different fellowship—one that was much closer to my home, so I moved that same week.

As a new believer, I was always looking for an opportunity to pray for anyone who was in need of a healing, or wanted a prophetic word from God. I do not know why I prayed as I did. Somehow, my prayers would spiritually hit home. Days later I was asked, "Do you remember the prayer you prayed for me?" I would always smile and say, "NO." Most of these individuals would then tell me everything was now ok. Due to my immaturity, I was unaware I was experiencing special favor with God when it came to praying for others. I was unaware others did not have the same level of response in their prayer life. I have learned that the more time I spend with the Lord in His Word, the greater clarity I receive in prayer. I asked God why there were times when I totally missed it. His reply was, "Your pride gets in the way and I hate the smell of pride." From that day, forward I did my best to pray and not get into pride (Proverbs 11:2).

Here is an example of my prayers. Our church had a family who were farmers. I had limited natural knowledge concerning their needs and that is how I began my prayer. Although the state was experiencing a drought, I asked God to give them a bumper crop that year. I asked that none of their farm equipment would break down and that all their vehicles would get exceptional oil and gas mileage. His wife wanted a job that would enable her to be at home when their children got home from school each day.

Eight months later Mr. "Ur" gave a testimony about all the things God had done for his family. To my surprise, God had met each request. I do not want to sound like their blessings were totally due to my praying. I am sure Mr. and Mrs. "Ur" had been praying for the same outcome.

During my first five years as a believer, I had not heard any teachings concerning a word of knowledge, faith, gifts of healings, the working of miracles, prophecy, discerning of spirits, different kinds of tongues, or interpretation of tongues. Another pastor, whom I was now sitting under, explained I had been moving in some of these spiritual gifts. He loaned me several books that clarified the workings and the gifts of the Holy Spirit. That same year, the Holy Spirit revealed to me that all gifts are rooted in the Seven Spirits of God (Isaiah 11:1-2; Romans 12:6-8; 1 Corinthians 12:8-11; Ephesians 4:11).

That week I became a "Holy Spirit Junkie." If I heard of anyone moving in the gifts of the Spirit, I wanted to be there to hear what God was saying and doing. I did not just want to see what God was doing; I wanted to participate in what God was doing. There were times when I heard the name of a minister that I would have a quickening in my spirit and know that it would be beneficial for me to pursue their meetings or read their books. Eventually, I found a prophetic teacher I enjoyed—only his program came on at 5 a.m.

It did not matter; I was spiritually hungry. I got up every morning at 4:30 a.m. to watch this prophetic television evangelist. All he did was talk about money, which made me angry and caused me to wonder why. I had never realized that money was my god. I did not want to believe what I was hearing in my spirit man.

You do not have to be rich to worship money; you can be poor or middle class and have money as your god. God revealed that money was a god in my life and I was determined to get free of this "Yenom demon" as well as any other non–Christian behavior. The "Yenom demon" is an evil spirit that mentally twists, bends and distorts all money issues making everything appear backwards. It makes a person think they never have enough money, which is a distorted view. Years ago, I received the revelation concerning the spelling of the word "MONEY." Reverse the letters and they spell the name of the demon "Yenom" and that is why I call it by that name. I have had the privilege of cancelling the curse of the "Yenom demon" from many individuals, freeing those who had been bound all of their life.

That same week the Holy Spirit gave me a revelation concerning the threefold cord, which will give any believer a spiritual breakthrough when they use ALL three cords. When I applied the three cords, I obtained freedom and I have continued to walk in that freedom to this day.

One of the ancient symbols of the trinity is the threefold cord. The threefold cord symbolizes God the Father, God the Son and God the Holy Spirit. They are three separate individuals and yet they are the same individual. In other words, they are inseparable, equal persons and indivisibly One God. All three of these cords are in the gospel of Matthew chapter six.

"Take heed that you do not do your charitable deeds of {**GIVING**} before men, to be seen by them. Otherwise, you have no reward from your Father in heaven. Therefore, when you do a charitable deed, do not sound a trumpet before you as the hypocrites do in the synagogues and in the streets, that they may have glory from men. Assuredly, I say to you, they have their reward. But when you do a charitable deed, do not let your left hand know what your right hand is doing, that your charitable deed may be in secret; and your Father who sees in secret will Himself reward you openly" (Matthew 6:1-4).

The body of Christ needs to be set free in the area of giving, especially money, which is their tithes and free will offerings. I to needed freedom in this area, which would enable me to move on with God. I needed freedom and revelation especially in the realm of understanding tithes and offerings. The second cord is in the next three verses.

"And when you {**PRAY**}, you shall not be like the hypocrites. For they love to pray standing in the synagogues and on the corners of the streets, that they may be seen by men. Assuredly, I say to you, they have their reward. But you, when you pray, go into your room, and when you have shut your door, pray to your Father who is in the secret place; and your Father who sees in secret will reward you openly, when you pray, do not use vain repetitions as the heathen do. For they think that they will be heard for their many words" (Matthew 6:5-7).

These three verses specifically speak of praying and being more effective by doing it in secret. That is without anyone knowing what you are wanting from God. The last of these threefold cords is in verses sixteen through eighteen.

"Moreover, when you {**FAST**}, do not be like the hypocrites, with a sad countenance. For they disfigure their faces that they may appear to men to be fasting. Assuredly, I say to you, they have their reward. But you, when you fast, anoint your head and wash your face, so that you do not appear to men to be fasting, but to your Father who is in the secret place; and your Father who sees in secret will reward you openly" (Matthew 6:16-18).

This powerful revelation on fasting ties the knot in the threefold cord. It was the crowning of the first two. This is what gives power to our giving and to our prayers. These three cords, when done correctly, will add greatly to your spiritual bank account and reap great dividends. I began laying up treasure for myself in heaven, where neither moth nor rust destroys and where thieves do not break in and steal. For where your treasure is, there your heart will be also (Matthew 6:19-21).

We make spiritual deposits into our bank account in heaven when we give to the poor and needy, when we pray in secret for the needs of others and when we fast with unselfish motives.

Karah has taught about these threefold cords at Women's Aglow meetings, explaining that our fasting is like putting icing on the cake. This really gets the Fathers attention. Our giving, praying and fasting as Matthew says is a sure recipe for spiritual success.

The Holy Spirit also revealed that each of these verses contains a different degree of authority and power. Giving elevates you to the "some thirty (30)" which produces **faith**. The majority of the church is operating with 30 % power. Could this be why we have so many weak believers?

When you add prayer to your giving, you have stepped up to the "some sixty (60)" which produces **hope**. There is a small majority in the church whose lives are always at the line of victory and yet they never have the power to cross over into a greater anointing. Are these the individuals who volunteer for every position and duty that comes available in the church?

When you combine giving and praying with the final action of fasting you will then enter into the "some a hundred (100)" fold return which produces **love** (Mark 4:8). Almost every fellowship has someone who moves in power and authority. Often it is the little old grandma giving, praying and fasting on a consistent basis.

My freedom came when I began to activate the threefold cords of Matthew chapter six. These three cords of grace are similar to three stepping stones; we can stand on any of them individually and go nowhere. By Gods grace when we give correctly, pray correctly and fast correctly we will go forth and make disciples of all nations.

Prophetic Hunger

I really enjoyed watching the prophetic television evangelist when he prayed for the sick or cast out demons. No one in my city was doing either of the ministries that I desired to learn. One morning this evangelist motioned for a man to come up onto the platform. The man was deaf in both ears. When the evangelist commanded the foul deaf spirit to come out, in Jesus name, the man could hear and became so overwhelmed he began to cry out of sheer joy.

In the past, whenever I prayed for a person I only asked for a healing and never cast out a demon. What I saw that morning changed the way I ministered.

I had opened my own plumbing company and was my only employee. One Sunday afternoon, I received a call from a first time customer. Upon arriving at his house, I noticed he had a hearing aid in his left ear. When I inquired about his hearing he said, "I am totally deaf in my right ear, and have 50% hearing loss in the left ear. All the men in my family go deaf at the age of fifty."

He paid me for the repairs, but before I turned to walk away, I asked him if he would allow me to pray for his hearing? After pausing for a brief moment, he agreed and stepped forward. I had him remove the hearing aid from his left ear. I then placed my two index fingers into his ears and commanded the foul deaf spirit to come out, in Jesus name. When I removed my fingers, tears began streaming down his face as he heard the birds in the trees across the street—something he could not do before. The man received his miracle (Mark 16:17; Luke 10:17).

I became excited and asked if he would come to the evening service and tell the people what Jesus had done for him. Suddenly he became angry and ordered me off his property. Puzzled, I asked if he knew God, which was strange, because I never ask a person if they know God (Hebrews 8:11; James 2:19). I always ask if they remember the day they accepted Jesus Christ as their personal Savior.

He shouted, "Yes, I know God, I am the head Rabbi at the new Jewish synagogue." I said, "You better give thanks to the Lord Jesus Christ for your healing." He waved his hand in the air, turned and walked off. Weeks later, I saw the same man shopping and noticed that he had put his hearing aide back into his ear. He had lost his miracle. His heart would not allow him to give glory where the glory was due. When we publically testify of our healing, we are solidifying our faith in the Lord Jesus Christ, His marvelous grace, mercy, and compassion—by the way, Jesus drives a **G.M.C.** pickup, powered, by His **G**race, **M**ercy and **C**ompassion.

Tongues & Interpretation

As a new Christian, I had stood in over one hundred prayer lines to receive the Baptism of the Holy Spirit with the evidence of speaking in other tongues (1 Corinthians 12:10). I have often joked about my hair falling out because I had so many hands laid on my head. The hairs on my head are so few that God has now named them all.

During those years, I became frustrated over not receiving the gift of tongues. I had patiently stood in very long prayer lines only to leave disappointed many times. I remember one instance in particular where a deacon standing to my right kept saying, "Hold on brother just hold on;" while at the same time, a second deacon was standing to my left saying, "Let it go brother and let God." Everyone seemed to have a different way to receive the baptism of the Holy Spirit, yet nothing ever happened for me. As I was leaving a man told me to pray more and another man said I must ask in faith and do not doubt.

I had gotten so discouraged with trying to enter into this blessing that I threw up my hands and said, "God if You are going to give me this gift of other tongues, I do not want it unless You also give me the gift of interpretation of tongues with it." I had forgotten about my prayer and sometime during the next few weeks, as I was driving down the highway all of a sudden these three words came out of my mouth "Teak-Ah-Low" (spelled phonically). The moment they came out, I heard a voice behind me say, "Jesus is Lord!" With stammering lips and another tongue, I was praising the Lord (Isaiah 28:11).

I just about lost control of my van; I was so excited that I did not know what to do. For the rest of the day I must have said those three words a thousand times. We must remember, "All supernatural gifts are given." Gifts are given and the fruit is grown by those who have been given the gift. In other words, you will have to develop your gift whether the gift is a natural gift or a supernatural gift. You must hone, refine and sharpen whatever gifts God has given you. This only comes through using them every chance you have and constantly bathing in the word of God.

I had read numerous books and heard about twenty sermons during the early years of my Christian walk concerning those called to the end time ministry. In addition, countless times others have told me that my call is specifically to the end time ministry. I have had many open visions concerning what a small portion of those glorious days will be like. I know I am only one of many people in the earth who has this wonderful calling.

I have heard of the reoccurring visions that Brother Paul had, describing the end time move of God, which represent worldwide salvations. These salvations will be so great in number that "It will appear as if the entire world had become saved." Of course, it will only appear as if all have received salvation because of the vast numbers. I have sensed deep within my spirit that during this particular period, the same angel of the Lord will once again stand next to me. I believe this time, I will be able to see the angel as well as hear and repeat word for word whatever he says.

Brother Who

Later that week I took my pastor to a steak house for lunch in celebration of me getting the gift of other tongues. As we waited for our meal, the name of a local pastor came up in our conversation. I asked, "what is God going to do with Brother _ _ _ _ _?" My pastor said, "who knows what God is going to do with Brother _ _ _ _ _?" At that time an audible voice came from the end of our table saying, "Yes, what is God going to do with Brother _ _ _ ?" That encounter made my pastor jump out of his seat. He began inquiring if anyone sitting near our table had said those words. No one that is a human being had said those words. That was quite an experience for my friend.

"Supernatural Mark"

Years ago, a prophetic minister walked up to me and said, "Do not be slothful but become a follower of those who through faith and patience inherited the promises of God" (Hebrews 6:12). My mother had told me everyone in the delivery room, including her, saw the "Supernatural Mark" that appeared on the crown of my head during my birth. The doctor began to write down the Hebrew words when the star and the writing disappeared. During the past years, I have had relatives as well as total strangers walk up to me and say, "Be faithful until death and you will receive the crown of life" (Revelation 2:10).

I had heard so much from my mother concerning the "Supernatural Mark," I actually became annoyed by the very idea of it. That is when I asked several of my close friends in the ministry about their opinion of the "Supernatural Mark." They were puzzled and did not have an answer. One said it all sounded foolish and perhaps my mother was delusional at the time of my birth. This was no help at all so I kept asking God to reveal to me if this was for real or a foolish tale. I prayed about this Supernatural Mark for several years before the answer came.

I had spent five days in fasting and prayer prior to a Morning Star prophetic conference. During that time, I had asked God to validate the "Supernatural Mark." While at the 1996 Harvest Conference my answer came. The evening ministry session had ended and we were to close by ministering to one another. The room had around 3000 conference attendees. It was impossible to walk in any direction without bumping into another person. Looking up, I noticed a man on the opposite side of the main conference room approximately 80 feet away. It was as if our eyes locked on each other and within seconds he was standing in front of me. Reaching out, he placed his right hand on my left shoulder and said, "God wants to settle an issue with you once and for all."

The next thing I knew, the Holy Spirit carried my spirit upwards. I found myself overhead looking down on a portion of the conference attendees. At that exact moment, I saw the man who was praying for me. Then I saw the "Supernatural Mark." I could see the six–pointed star; it was dark purple in color and the writing was a deep blue— almost black. At that same moment the man said, "Good you saw it;" he removed his hand from my shoulder, turned, and walked away. I glanced downwards at the floor in total shock for a second or two. When I looked up, the man was nowhere to be seen; he had disappeared. Could he have been an angel? I do not know (Hebrews 13:2).

For a long time I have felt in my spirit that there is a generation of believers in the earth who will walk in the same anointing, gifting, and calling the Lord has commissioned in me. I advise everyone to ask God for the best He has for your life. Do not ask or settle for "His good will" or "His acceptable will" but only for "His perfect will" (Romans 12:2). You must be willing to sacrifice anything and everything God asks you to give up in order to walk in His perfect word, will and way for your life. I wish to clarify that God WILL NOT ask you to divorce your spouse and leave your children to follow Him. If God tells you to move, you take your family with you. I have heard it said, If God calls a man, He will call the woman also.

I personally believe this is a misleading notion and an incorrect statement. God does not call the wife just because He has called her husband, nor does He call the husband just because He has called his wife. There are many men and women called into the ministry and their spouses are not, other than to support what God has instructed them to do.

I have heard of marriages falling apart and ending in divorce because of the foolish idea that both are ministers or neither are ministers. If your spouse does not feel called, allow them to come and support what you are doing. Do not force them or put a guilt trip on them for not wanting to be a platform speaker.

I thank God that my wife is a minister called to "The Good News Gospel" and she is an excellent speaker.

She has saved my bacon many times. Our gifts and calling complement each other. I have no problem in obtaining revelation and at times I fall short on the interpretation and application portion. My wife's strongest gift is in the areas of interpretation and application. Every week someone calls wanting her to interpret a dream or a vision. What is excellent about my wife's gifts is that her prayers impart and stir up these same gifts in others.

Laying on of hands

One day, as I was pulling out of my driveway, I was strongly impressed that I would meet an anointed woman. As a plumber, I never knew for whom or where I would be working from day to day. My first job was for a Christian schoolteacher who had just moved to Texas from New York State. She commented that since moving to our city she had begun experiencing nightmares, which was something she never had before.

The conversation quickly went back to her house and the needed repairs. As she pointed out damaged spots, I could not help but notice the anointing that flashed from her hands as she made gestures in different directions pointing out what she wanted repaired (Habakkuk 3:4). She certainly had the anointing and the gift of "The Laying on of Hands" for those who are in need (Mark 16:18; Acts 8:17; Hebrews 6:2).

We use the term "The Laying on of Hands" so freely we have lost its true power. In reality it is an anointed gift and ministry, in fact it is a very special gift. (I personally believe that the body of Christ has lost this precious gift during the dark ages). She is the only person I have ever met with that specific anointed gift and calling of "The Laying on of Hands." Although I have often used the term, "The Laying on of Hands," that day I learned I did not know as much as I thought about the gift of "The Laying on of Hands."

After completing everything on her list and collecting for the job, I asked if I could speak a blessing over her house before I left. Quickly, she graciously agreed to my request. As I stood in the hallway praying I glanced into the front bedroom and to my surprise, a spirit of death was standing there in the middle of the room. I nonchalantly said, "Spirit of death I release you from your assignment in Jesus name Amen." As I turned to leave, she grabbed my arm and asked, "what do you mean by "spirit of death I release you from your assignment. I want to know, now tell me." I explained that a "Spirit of Death" was standing in the front bedroom and all I did was tell it to go, it was that simple. I did not know why it was there. I assured her it was no longer there. It was easy to see she was not pleased with my statement, but I had to leave to complete my other jobs.

Three months later, I found myself back at that same house doing another repair job. Upon entering the home, I was shocked. The woman had hung religious crosses, candles or photos in every room. When I commented about this strange form of decorating she said, "I do not want any demons or spirits of death coming back to this house. Then she began telling me what she had found out about the house through inquires with the neighbors.

As it turned out, the house had been vacant and for sale for over five years. No one wanted to buy it because of the ugly exterior color as well as all the repairs that were needed. She said that after I left, for the next several days she went door to door to every house on her street inquiring about the previous owner. She learned the house had belonged to a retired man who had died six years earlier. The police had found his decayed body in the front bedroom.

Before leaving, I cancelled the spirit of fear that had come against her. After the prayer, it looked as if a light had gone off in her spirit man. Her continence became brighter than before. Several months later, she called my office to tell me she had removed the religious items and she was no longer having any nightmares.

God does not give individual phobias, fears, and nightmares; these come from the devil. Much of the time there is a connection with some type of witchcraft. You need to know, that to encounter witchcraft, you do not have to go to a witch or to a witchdoctor.

Witchcraft comes through psychic readers, Ouija boards, palm readers, tarot cards, eight balls, fortunetellers, and crystal ball readers, as well as our news media, horoscopes, movies, spiritual or magic board games etc...

The worst spirits released are through an American tradition called Halloween along with the Ouija board. There is NO such thing as a good witch, or a white witch, or good witchcraft, or white witchcraft. It does not matter what color you color them—black, white, pink, yellow, red, green, etc., all witches and witchcraft are of the devil. It does not matter if you call them good or nice. The word of God calls them evil and their words and work are sin. As I was watching a television show about magic, I heard the Holy Spirit say "The Devil and His Group Works Magic." "I Perform Miracles." Remember, all magic is an illusion and a counterfeit of Gods true miracles.

"There shall not be found among you ...who casts a spell {or works magic}...For whoever does these things is detestable to the Lord; and because of these detestable things the Lord your God will drive them out before you" (Deuteronomy 18:10-13).

King Saul went to the house of the Witch Endor, a woman with a familiar spirit. Because he knew better, King Saul lost his kingdom and he later committed suicide (1Samuel 8). All familiar spirits are not of God; they are of the devil.

Bed Wetting

I was in the middle of a repair job when it became evident that the woman of the house had a problem. She began crying, shaking, and talking to herself. Because I was in the same room as she, there was no way she could hide her actions. I asked if there was anything I might do to help. Looking up, she apologetically said, "Forgive me; I do not know what to do. My daughter has a bed–wetting problem and at times it gets the best of me. Every day I wash sheets and I am tired of it. We are faithful Christians and I do not know why this is happening to us."

I told her I wet the bed until I was thirteen and then the Lord delivered me and He will deliver your daughter of bed–wetting if you let Him.

For a minute, she stood there speechless with a blank stare on her face. Then she said, "I have nothing to lose; my daughter gets home from school in about two hours."

I told her that her daughter did not need to be present for deliverance. All I needed to do was to lay my hand on her daughter's bed. She led me to a bedroom decorated with children's scenes painted on bright pink and yellow walls. Walking over to the bed, I placed my right hand on the pillow and commanded "The Spirit of Fear" to leave in Jesus name. Turning to the mother I said, "It is done, she will be delivered the moment she lays her head on her pillow. I will now go back and fix your faucet."

She stood there with an even greater look of bewilderment on her face. She asked, "What is done? What do you mean?

Smiling I said, "Your daughter will never wet the bed again." When I finished her repair job, she reluctantly thanked me for my prayer on her daughter's behalf. She paid my bill, and I left.

Four months later, this same customer called needing another faucet repaired. Within minutes of arriving at the home, the first words out of her mouth were, "Do you remember the first time you came to my home and prayed for my daughter's problem?"

"Yes I do I replied,"

"Well she has not wet the bed since the day you prayed over her bed."

I spent a few minutes explaining that the anointing of God is transferable through fabric and that was why I laid my hand on her daughter's pillow. Fear is a Generational Curse. In this particular situation, the fear was from witchcraft (2 Timothy 1:7). I warned her about the family playing with things such as Ouija boards and tarot cards. In addition, I highly recommended they stop honoring Halloween, which is Satan's High Holy Day.

Witchcraft

I had a personal encounter with witchcraft in 1969, the year I graduated from High School. Between the years of 1969 and 1979, I was involved in over twenty auto accidents. It became so bad my friends did not want me to ride in the same vehicle with them. One time, I was in three auto accidents in two days. None of these accidents were my fault, but each time, two automobiles received damage, and I was injured.

I was in an explosion that hospitalized me for over a month. I encountered electric shocks twice so badly that I was unable to work for several days. Three times I fell off high roofs and once I even fell through a roof.

When I came under the "Blood Covenant" of the Lord Jesus Christ on February 10, 1979, the auto accidents ceased. At that time, the only thing I did not understand was the spiritual connection between His Blood Covenant and me. As a young believer, I was glad for His hand of safety over my life although I did not fully understand everything there was to know about the blood covenant.

For some reason, many small, less dangerous things kept happening even though I kept praying and believing things would get better. One thing that kept bothering me was that I had been a faithful believing Christian and was constantly being injured. This was not what I call an "Overcoming Christian Life." The word bad is perhaps not strong enough...It was dreadful! I had become fearful and paranoid with myself. At one time in my life, I did not want to ride in the same vehicle with me either. I would wake up and wonder what was going to happen that day. I always prayed for God's best. He had given it, but I somehow missed getting hold of it. I felt I had not yet received it.

The church I was attending had invited a group of deliverance ministers to teach on inner healing. It was going to be hands on teaching and I was one of the first to volunteer. At the time, I did not see a great need for the teaching until all the teaching sessions were over. The session began with the lead minister anointing me with oil and a short prayer of rededication. During my ministry session, one of the ministers said, "A Spirit of Witchcraft had been assigned against you sometime in 1969. The assignment was to kill you; I see a spirit of death."

Wow, now that got my attention. The moment he said those words, I saw in the spirit realm a "lit black candle." I did not know what that meant, but another minister saw what looked like an African witchdoctor releasing curses and chants. The two ministers cancelled the assignment of death that was over me and deliverance came. The burdens were removed and the yoke destroyed and crushed because of the anointing oil (Isaiah 10:27).

Although I did not feel anything in the natural, I knew God was about to intervene in my life. Over the next few days, it became obvious to all that the black cloud that had followed me for over fifteen years had finally blown away. I have not had any more accidents. Praise God. During these past thirty plus years, I have learned that nothing, nothing, can stand in the way of a believer who desires to follow and obey the word, will and way of God.

One day several months later as I was sitting at an intersection waiting for the light to turn green, I specifically asked, "Lord, where did that curse against me come from?" I immediately had a vision of a certain place. I turned my van around and drove to the location I saw in my vision and was amazed at what I saw. There was a four-foot square sign on the front of the building with the words, "Palm Reader & Tarot Cards" painted in florescent red. The Bible warns us this is a major sin.

"There shall not be found among you anyone who makes his son or his daughter pass through the fire, or one who practices witchcraft, or a soothsayer, or one who interprets omens, or a sorcerer, or one who conjures spells {or works magic}, or a medium, or a spiritualist, or one who calls up the dead. For all who do these things are an abomination to the Lord, and because of these abominations the Lord your God drives them out from before you" (Deuteronomy 18:10-13).

The word abomination is defined as "anything that arouses strong disgust; a revolting thing; a loathing, hatred of, strong dislike for, or detestable." Do you now see how any act of sorcery is an abomination unto God?

In simple terms, Christians are not to seek any type of spiritual advice from witches, wizards, soothsayers, fortunetellers, warlocks, sorcerers, anyone who conjures spells, mediums, spiritualist, or one who calls up the dead. Many Christian's cross this spiritual line by getting their fortunes read, by calling a psychic hot line, or reading the horoscope page before making a decision.

That led me to a second question I asked God, "Who would have paid to have a curse of death put against me?" I immediately had a second vision. I saw the state of Arkansas and the mother of my girlfriend. The mother went into the very same building I had seen in the open vision. She paid a witch to release a spirit of death against me. I understood why the mother would have done such a thing. Her daughter, who I was dating, had a miserable home life and wanted us to get married and I did not want to get married.

Since I was against the idea of marriage and was one of the only friends the girl had, she attempted suicide.

I went to her job, found her passed out, and rushed her to the hospital where she remained for several weeks.

To this day, I feel sorry for anyone who hates another individual so badly that he or she would go to a witch's house to have a hex, curse or death spell placed on the person in question. There is greater power in God; however, we must not think there is no power in the demonic assignments spoken in and through witchcraft. The devil always attacks those next in line for promotion.

I asked God to forgive the woman who had the curse put against me and save the entire household by the blood of the Lamb. Amen.

Hidden Treasure

There was a season I begged God to give me the ability to witness and lead people to His Son. One day, I heard down in my spirit; ask if they remember any important event in their life? Armed with that information, I set out to witness. I wanted to develop any additional skills that would be useful to win souls to Christ. I soon realized if an individual could remember when they obtained their license, graduated from school or college, but could NOT remember the time they accepted Jesus as their personal Savior they had never made the commitment.

I have also learned that commitment is an area most men avoid. In fact when leading men to Christ, I realized if I used the word commitment they lingered a great deal longer in their decision. Yet if I used the word pledge or oath, they were more willing to say yes to salvation.

In order for you to comprehend the rest of this story, you must grasp the understanding of how I witness. I always ask the person "Do you remember a time when you received your driver's license, or married, or moved?" I use whatever I think they will say yes to and then I ask them, "Do you remember a time when you personally asked Jesus Christ to come into your heart." If they have to think on the second part of the question, there is a good chance they are not saved. To be born again is a major thing for anyone. God does not accidentally save a person. Salvation is a deliberate action on an individual's part. It is a request. It is a deliberate action of thought and consideration. Your parents may have given you to God at birth or at a baby dedication but that does not save you. The day will come when you will have to make a decision on your own. No one can receive salvation for another person.

"Therefore I make known to you that no one speaking by the Spirit of God calls Jesus accursed, and no one can say that Jesus is Lord except by the Holy Spirit" (1 Corinthians 12:3).

In other words, no one can say Jesus Christ is Lord unless that person has the Holy Spirit and if that person has the Holy Spirit they have received eternal salvation by the blood and the cross of the Lord Jesus Christ (1 Corinthians 12:3).

One day, at a plumbing repair job at a rental house, I realized I had a perfect opportunity to witness when the renter passed through the kitchen and went outside to sit on the back steps to have a cigarette (smoking will not send you to hell but it will make you smell as if you have been there.) I hurriedly glued all the fittings and as they were drying, I went out to witness to her. Instead of asking my usual question, I opened my mouth and out came the following words, "Do you know Jesus?" That was not the way I witnessed and I immediately wondered why I said what I had.

This woman was in her late twenties, very frail in appearance and spoke with an extremely soft voice. In fact, the first time I spoke with her, I could hardly hear what she said. When I asked the question "Do you know Jesus" she turned her head to look at me and both eyeballs rolled up somewhere into the back of her head displaying two glassy white eyeballs. Her light, frail voice disappeared as she answered; "YES I KNOW JESUS" in a deep masculine voice, as the sides of her mouth began to drool with saliva along with a foul odor gushing out of her mouth with each word she spoke. Then, just as quickly, her eyes reappeared in the sockets where they had disappeared moments earlier.

I decided to try a different approach, so I asked her to tell me about her religious upbringing or any kind of religious meetings she had attended. In her normal soft voice, she said, "Well my dad is a Hindu, my mother is of another Eastern religion, my brother and his wife are Mormons, but my husband is a Jehovah Witness; and I have attended all of their meetings at one time or another." She went on to say that she had not felt led to personally join any of them.

After hearing all of that, I nearly fell off the porch. I asked her if she would like to renounce her involvement with ALL of these false religious cult groups and become a Christian. She replied, "No, I am perfectly happy with my life now, maybe at some other time thank you."

I decided not to do a deliverance. She was not going to become a Christian and if I had cast out the demons, the end would have been even worse for her. When an unclean spirit goes out of a person, it goes through dry places, seeking rest, and finds none. Eventually that spirit will attempt to return to the house of the person from which it came. When it returns to that person it takes seven other spirits more wicked than itself, and they enter and dwell there. The latter state of that person is worse than the first (Matthew 12:43-45).

At one time in my life, I was a hotshot prophetic minister and did not realize that without discernment I would cause major mental anxiety to an individual just to make me look good. The Lord has spent countless hours training me on how to grow up as a more mature prophetic minister and to discern spiritually "What to do or What Not to Do." He did not give up on me nor will He give up on you. We are all in school. It is spiritual education, known as "Training for Reigning." It was during this time the Lord was teaching me how NOT to bury my time, treasure or talents. Thank you, Jesus.

The apostle Paul said that the spirit of the prophet is subject to the prophet (1 Corinthians 14:32). In other words, a prophetic person does not have to give all they hear or see. They must learn to use discernment and know when to release a word and when to keep back the word of the Lord.

Here is a twenty five year old example of how I was a stupid hotshot prophetic minister. One time a customer asked me to move my van to the front of her house and use the front door because of a delivery she was expecting. Wasting no time, I moved my van and upon entering the home, I glanced over into a sunken living room area. Standing at the far end of the room was a spirit of suicide. The woman of the house had let me in and was walking several feet in front of me. I popped off by saying, "Hey someone committed suicide in that room."

Stopping cold in her tracks, she turned and faced me with tears beginning to run down one cheek. She said, "My husband hung himself two years ago on Christmas Eve there in the living room. I do not use that room anymore because every time I enter it I feel as if something evil is present."

If I could have found a hole to crawl into, I would have. I tried to apologize but it did little good. I did not know what to do to correct what I had so foolishly said to her. When I commented about a spirit of suicide, I felt powerful to know such things. Now I felt like the stupidest human on earth. I asked her to forgive me for my foolish declaration. I then stepped down into the pit of the living room and was now on level ground with the spirit of suicide. I commanded the suicidal spirit to leave and never return to that home. As the words were coming out of my mouth, a cold wind blew throughout the entire room; the curtains began to move from side to side and within minutes the temperature of the room returned to normal.

I then asked for the spirit of peace to come and fill the entire house—especially the living room. I declared that the sunken room was no longer sunken but was now a container for the peace and presence of the Lord God to dwell in. Amen.

I asked the woman of the house to step down into the living room and tell me if she still felt an evil presence. Upon entering the same area where I was standing, she commented she could feel a peace she had never remembered feeling in that room. After I completed the plumbing job, I went to my prayer closet at the bay front and spent some quality time before the Lord repenting for my stupidity.

"Father God, as You revealed to me many, who are reading this book are going to a higher level of accountability in the prophetic with a greater anointing. I ask you to put a hedge of protection around them and do not allow any of them to make the same mistakes I have made. I ask Your Holy Spirit of Promise to open their eyes of discernment and understanding in all things. Release the Holy Fire of Your anointing to burn up all wood, hay and stubble. Purge these into vessels of precious gold and silver fit for the Lords use in Jesus name Amen (2 Timothy 2:20).

Time, Treasure & Talents

I want to return to the subject of burying one's time, treasure or talents. Here is a little something for you the Lord shared with me. From out of the dust of the earth all are created; the day will come when we shall return to the dust of the earth (Ecclesiastes 3:20). When people bury any of their talents in the earth, they have actually buried their talents within themselves. Therefore, people who bury their talent or talents within themselves will never use them and are accountable to their creator for their fearful slothfulness. Scripture is clear. Everyone receives both natural and spiritual talents; in the parable one received five talents, another two, and another one—each according to his or her own ability. A day is appointed when everyone will have to give an account of their talents; either they will receive more as a reward or have the few in their possession taken away because of their slothfulness (Matthew 25:15-30).

Our time, treasure and talents are only a small portion of the treasures that are within these earthen vessels. Our spiritual talents are worth far more than any gold, silver, or precious stones that are in the earth. The Kingdom of God is not in word but in power (1 Corinthians 4:20). Our time, treasure, and talents are for others; we are not to hoard our treasures on ourselves.

We have this treasure in earthen vessels that the Excellency of the power may be of God, and not of us (2 Corinthians 4:7). We have this ministry as we have received mercy; we do not lose heart for God has given to us the ministry of reconciliation (2 Corinthians 4:1; 5:18).

Wherever your heart is, there you will find your treasure also. Your treasure is the Kingdom of God within. It is your gifts and callings that God through the Holy Spirit deposited within you before your birth (Jeremiah 1:5). These gifts and callings become empowered by the Holy Spirit when you received salvation. As we work out our own salvation, we will discover our place in the body of Christ (Philippians 2:12). We will never possess what we are unwilling to passionately pursue. A portion of our discovery is learning how to minister within the realm of our gifts and calling. It is impossible to separate your spiritual treasures from your calling they go hand in hand. For where your treasure is, there your heart will be also (Matthew 6:21). This verse reveals that our gift of God should be our hearts desire. What has your heart yearned to do?

I had a vision once where I was a piece of cold hard steel the Lord placed into a flaming furnace. The steel became cherry red; it then was removed and placed on the anvil of life. The word of God hammered the steel and fashioned it into the wordsmith's desires then it was plunged into a silver and gold vessel of living water, which tempered it to His desired strength (Jeremiah 23:29; Philippians 3:21).

The candlelight in your earthen vessel comes from the illumination of the glory of God or the Holy Spirit that is within you. The word of God is a lamp candle unto our feet and a search light unto our path (Psalms 110:105). The more of the word of God you get into you, the greater the illumination of His light you will have to walk with. I have heard people say they want to get into the word of God. It is better for the word of God to get in you. Respect the word of God and you will attract it to you. The spirit of a man is the lamp of the Lord, that is earching all the inner depths of his heart (Proverbs 20:27).

If you will eat the word, you will become the word. When you want something you have never had, you have to do something you have never done. Because I am called by the name of the Lord God of hosts, I will find His words and eat them, and then they will become joy and rejoicing in my heart (Jeremiah 15:16). My daily routine is eating His word, which lays the foundation for my future. God honors every free will offering and sacrifice I give to Him. The greater my offering or sacrifice the greater my reward. I will only possess what I will passionately pursue.

God already knows what is in everyone's heart. It is His desire for everyone to come to the same realization. God wants everyone to ask His help to remove anything that will hinder his or her personal walk or relationship with Him. There is nothing too big or too small that God is not interested in when it comes to one of His children.

Fragrances

As a young boy, my brother and I tormented red ants. I would locate the ant bed by smelling the ants. I thought everyone could smell ants and I thought it was strange that at times when I was around certain individuals I would smell ants. Five years after my radical conversion I learned that ants were symbolic of the gift of wisdom (Proverbs 6:6). I soon realized when I smelled ants on an individual, it revealed the individual had the gift of wisdom.

Throughout the years, the Holy Spirit has expanded my understanding on fragrances. Every gift and calling of God has its own sound, color and fragrance. When I teach on this I use the cliché "I Smell a Rat" in reference to something that is not right. I use this illustration in hopes my listeners will grasp what I am teaching; all our senses, whether either spiritual or natural, have a level of discernment. We must hone our gifts to bring them to the highest level of use.

The fragrance of a banana indicates a gift of evangelism; the fragrance of a pineapple indicates the gift of hospitality; the fragrance of a peach, indicates a person who is a problem solver; the fragrance of an apple indicates the gift of teaching; the fragrance of flowers indicates the gift of intercession etc...

The evil one has smells and colors attached to his manifestations, sin stinks. At one time it became impossible for me to go to any public place because of the smell of sin, which stunk so badly, my eyes would begin to burn.

Once, in a meeting in Jacksonville Florida, Jesus walked into the room and the air filled with a wonderful fragrance of myrrh, aloes, and cassia. I asked if anyone in the room could smell anything. Several others did and were excited when I told them it was the fragrance from the robe of Jesus (Psalms 45:8).

The evil of the devil also smells, but it is not a sweet fragrance. His smell is always a horrible stinking smell. Sexual sins smell like dog manure. Lies smell like vomit etc...

Set Free

As I said earlier, the demonic realm also has a smell; however, they are not sweet fragrances. I hope that after reading this short example you will have a better understanding and will know what to do when you unexpectedly smell a demonic spirit.

All believers are kings and priest ("Kingdom Priest") unto God (Revelation 1:6). The priest went before the Ark of the Covenant blowing the trumpets (Joshua 6:13). Today, this (the blowing of trumpets) is the representation of the people of God decreeing prophetic declarations and warfare praises during a worship service.

Many times, I have been in the midst of an assembly during high praise worship and all of a sudden, I smelled cigarette smoke, marijuana, beer or some other form of alcohol. When this occurs, I command the demonic spirit to leave the building and not come back.

This is what has happened. Somewhere in the fellowship, an individual has obtained freedom from the demonic addiction like an addiction of nicotine and are rejoicing for the new freedom they have received (Nahum 1:7).

The demonic spirit of nicotine is now looking for a new home or individual to possess. If the demonic spirit finds an individual who is addicted to cigarettes, and attaches itself to that person, the individual's habit will increase to twice the amount they are presently smoking. The same stands true for all other forms of addictions.

If the individual who received the freedom from nicotine falls back into the addiction, the end will become worse than the first (Matthew 12:43-45; Luke 11:24-26).

Therefore, when you smell a rat in your worship service command it to leave your building and never come back. Your ability to smell and your spiritual discernment can go hand in hand.

An Exorcism

While living in the state of Arkansas a friend asked if I would give a high school senior a job. I was reluctant but agreed due to my friend's insistence. I picked up the student at his house, and before I left his driveway, I heard the Holy Spirit say, "Tell him some of the deliverance encounters you have experienced."

I began to reason within my heart, which was quite a wrestling match. I thought to myself, "This young man does not think very much of my belief in God now, and after I tell him about several encounters involving spiritual deliverances he will think that I'm a fruit cake." Nevertheless, I wanted to be obedient, so I began telling him about several very, very low level deliverances. By late afternoon, I had told him eight individual encounters.

We had three more jobs to do before we finished for the day. As I drove over to the job site, I asked him what he had thought about the deliverance stories. I was shocked with his reply.

"At the church I attend we really do not believe that demons exist today, especially in this modern age. All you have to do is quote Psalms 23 to solve any problem. If that did not work, you just quote the Lord's Prayer and that would solve whatever problem you may be experiencing. That is all anyone would ever have to do."

Those were the only verses he had memorized during his ten years as a believer. What a shame! He quit talking as we pulled onto the job site. A man met us at the door and showed us his plumbing problem. I sent my helper to the van for the extension ladder as I hooked up the electric cords.

As I began climbing up the ladder, the renter who had followed us into the back yard to watch suddenly fell to the ground. He began shaking and making sounds like he was moaning. I jumped down from the ladder and was going to command the demon to come out when I realized this was an ideal teaching situation. I calmly knelt beside the man and quoted Psalm 23. As I did, I looked over towards my helper and he nodded his head with approval. The man had no strength and needed help getting to his feet as he apologized for his actions.

I began to climb the ladder again, when the same thing occurred a second time. This time I knelt beside the man and quoted the Lord's Prayer. Once again, I looked towards my helper who gave me a big smile as he nodded his head in agreement. I felt badly for the man as he was very apologetic for his actions. I assured him everything would be ok. I helped the renter back to his feet and returned to my ladder.

The third time I went up the ladder much slower, knowing we were still going to have a demon manifest itself. The man again fell to the ground. This time he was rooting like a hog in the slimy mud and growling like a dog at the same time. Saliva was running out of both sides of his mouth with each bark and growl, while at the same time he emitted a foul odor. I was infuriated with the demon that was causing this entire situation. Jumping down from the ladder, I stood over the man and commanded the foul demonic spirit of pornography to come out of him and never enter again, "Be healed in Jesus name!" After all of this was over, the man stood to his feet by his own strength.

Looking over at me he said, "Wow! What was all that about? I feel great."

At that point, I led him in a rededication prayer, laid hands on him, and imparted the Holy Spirit.

Jesus has given to His believers who call upon His name, power over the enemy, and nothing shall hurt them (Luke 10:19).

I glanced over at my helper; his eyes were as large as saucers, his mouth was hanging wide open, and he had a rattled and confused look on his face. I went up on the roof and completed the plumbing job. As soon as we got back in the van, my helper said, "Take me home, you are crazy." The entire way back to his house, he trembled in fear. I offered to pray for him, but he did not want me to get anywhere near him.

During these past years, I have learned to teach with greater impact. If I had to do it over again I would have had my helper cast out the spirit even if I had to lead him one word at a time through the deliverance.

Christian Mystics

I had become interested in the early Christian Mystics when I realized there are many prophetic men and women of God moving in many of these same supernatural signs, wonders and miracles throughout America.

It was during this same time I first heard about Mr. Paul Cain who is considered by many to be one of the most anointed and accurate prophets in the world. I had obtained a video of him doing prophetic call out and every time I watched that video, the anointing of God came into my living room. I was so impressed with all I heard and saw involving his ministry, I began searching for a way to attend one of his conferences. I remembered the day I knelt down on my knees and said, aloud as well as in my heart, "Lord Jesus, if you will just have Mr. Cain call me out, I have the faith to step out and receive an anointing similar to his." When I stood to my feet, I felt that day would come. I had an inward conviction I was going to experience the supernatural on a much greater level than I ever imagined. I knew death and life are in the power of my tongue and because I love life, I will eat its fruit (Proverbs 18:20-21).

I have truly been satisfied from the fruit of my lips from eating the words of my mouth. For I found your words Lord God, and I did eat them; and your word was joy and rejoicing to me and to my heart: for by your name, O Lord God of hosts I am truly called.

I found myself constantly listening to audio tapes and praying aloud while I drove from job to job. At times I was so caught up in listening to the audio tapes I would find myself on the opposite side of town from where I had planned to go to because I was pondering verses or listening intently to the teaching.

Since witchcraft was now broken off my life, the blessings of God began to overshadow me. I was enjoying the "Lord's protection while driving and perhaps should have given my pickup some earthly attention. One afternoon, as I was hurrying across town I glanced down at my parts list to double check it. When I looked up from my list, I saw the back end of a semi-tractor trailer stopped in front of me. I was going thirty five miles per hour when I slammed on my breaks, but my brakes did not engage. Seconds before I would have hit the back of the parked semi trailer, an angel appeared, standing between our vehicles. He stretched forth his right hand and touched the hood of my pickup, which immediately came to a complete stop, and at the same time, shut off the pickup's motor. I blinked both eyes in amazement and rubbed them. I was expecting to see the angel still standing there when I looked a second time, but he was gone. He was like a bolt of lightning that flashed from out of nowhere and within a split second, he was gone. I sat there thinking about it for a few seconds, then I began to praise God for His supernatural protection. I knew He would give his angels charge over me to keep me in all His ways (Psalms 91:11; Luke 4:10).

Mark chapter 4 commands us not to tempt the Lord our God, so when I returned to my office, I promptly had my pickup delivered to the dealer for brake repairs. I think if I had not immediately taken care of the problem that was made known to me, I would have been tempting God. I still thank the Lord God Almighty for His mighty protection and deliverance that day and every day of my life.

A Wooden Spoon

As a plumber, I never knew from one day to the next what exciting adventure God had in store for me. I did not know if I was going to be used to lead someone into the kingdom of light, or if I was the vessel God would send to release His healing touch. I soon realized the Lord God mostly was using me to deliver and set the captive free. It made no difference, the pay was the same (1 Samuel 30:24) and I was enjoying my second job as a minister more than I ever imagined.

While living in Kansas City, I had a job at a very exclusive high–rise Condo. The moment I met the owner, I heard the Holy Spirit say, "This man is going to commit suicide after you leave." When I heard that, I had the man bring a kitchen chair into the living room and sit down. The moment he was seated the Lord God "Read His Mail."

I saw the good, the bad, and the ugly concerning all he had just encountered. (I want to make it clear that God did not reveal any of his sins to me.)

I was shocked when the word of knowledge, coupled with the prophetic word came forth for his life. It was an extremely high level giving the names of people and places. To make a very long story short, the man had determined to commit suicide by throwing himself off his thirteenth floor balcony because his girlfriend had given his engagement ring back to him, but kept the brand new Cadillac he had given her.

When the Holy Spirit began to reveal things it was evident that God had entered the room and the young man began to tremble. He received deliverance in five different areas where he had been afflicted since birth, all of which came through his bloodline. In addition, he rededicated his life to Jesus Christ and received the Holy Spirit with the evidence of speaking in other tongues. Before I left his Condo, he found his New Living Bible and I opened it to the New Testament and instructed him to remain in that portion of the Bible until the Holy Spirit directed him otherwise.

As I drove back home my heart was filled with the joy remembering if anyone wanders away from the truth whoever brings that sinner back will save that person from death and bring about the forgiveness of many sins (James 5:19-20). That night I could not sleep just knowing the Holy Spirit had intervened into his life snatching him out of a lukewarm lifestyle. God would not vomit this man's name out of His mouth nor blot his name out of the book of life. He was not lukewarm anymore (Revelation 3:5, 15, 16).

    I awoke the next morning to this same man calling. He had stayed up all night reading his Bible and was going to nap awhile before reading the New Testament for a second time. During the day I felt a little sorry for him, I knew his excitement would come under attack when he professed to his friends that he was no longer a lukewarm Christian. He was well off financially and had never experienced rejection until the day his girlfriend called off the engagement. I knew when he shared his new faith in Jesus with his wealthy family they would also reject him. Two weeks later the church he grew up in asked him to leave because they did not have a place for anyone like him. He was now a Holy Spirit filled, tongue talker in a traditional, mainline, denominational Church.

    This man's silver spoon had just become a wooden spoon. Wood always represents the cross of Jesus Christ. He was no longer eating from the silver spoon, which was his parent's perspective. He was now feeding himself daily from the word of God by a wooden spoon. He had chosen to take up his cross and follow Christ. Although he was on milk, at the rate he was advancing, it would not be long before he would be on solid food and spiritual meat (Hebrews 5:12-14).

    In Matthew chapter sixteen, Jesus said, "If any man or woman was going to follow Him, they would have to take up their own personal cross, and follow Him." Everyone's cross is different. It is impossible to carry someone else's cross and accomplish your life's calling. In

Luke chapter fourteen, Jesus declared that whosoever does not bear his or her own cross and follow Him cannot be His disciple. Disciples are people of determined discipline.

Daily Confessions

Jesus lives in the present tense. Jesus is the "I am." The gospels list over 88 references of Jesus declaring that He is the "I am." Today Jesus is still all we need. Yesterday is past and we cannot go back to alter anything. Tomorrow has not yet come and we have no guarantee we will be here to enjoy tomorrow.

A portion of the crucifixion given in John chapter nineteen reveals the crucifixion of three people. Two thieves were crucified, one on each side of Jesus. Golgotha was the place of the crucifixion, which was a hill that resembled a human skull. Everyone who is going to follow Jesus and become one of His disciples will have to crucify themselves in the place of their skull. The battle is in and over our mind. The mental realm is where we make the decisions that are good or evil, temporal or eternal. We all must have the same attitude Christ Jesus had, He humbled himself in obedience to God and died a criminal's death on a cross (Philippians 2:5-8).

The crucifixion of the two thieves is important to understand. The **first** thief's named was "Yesterday" (past tense). We cannot go back to yesterday to alter a single action or word. The devil wants to kill, steal and destroy whatever joyful memories we have from yesterday by implanting the words, "If only...!"

The **second** thief was named "Tomorrow" (future tense). Tomorrow never resides in the present. The devil wants to kill, steal and destroy our faith, hope and love by telling us to we wait until tomorrow to apologize, repent, believe in Jesus, or whatever it might be. The lie is that tomorrow, things will be better...! No! No! No! Speak up today; believe in His goodness today. Today is the first day of the rest of your life. Release active faith into your words today.

This is the reason why Jesus continuously declared that He was the "I am." Jesus is the here and now, the present tense. Today, if we will hear His voice, we will enter into His realm of "I am"!

During the height of my deliverance ministry, the economy began to go through a major slump. My work was down by 50%. At times, I had no work at all. For weeks on end, I did not even have a warranty job. When I was at the office of my accountant, she asked if I was going to close my doors and seek employment at a nearby base as so many others had done. Before I could answer her question, I heard these words come up from out of my spirit. "No way am I going to close my business! I have brought all my tithes into the storehouse and there will be food in my house. The Lord is opening the windows of heaven over me and is pouring out such a blessing I will not have enough room for it all for His words have not departed from my mouth. I have kept speaking them day and night and I will have good success" (Malachi 3:10; Joshua 1:8).

After leaving her office, I wondered why those verses came forth like that. Why did I make such a declaration? As I pondered those questions, I turned on the audio tape from Norvel Hayes. Although I had read many of his books this was the first time I had heard Brother Hayes. I found myself listening to that teaching tape five or six times that evening. The next day I listened to it ten more times. I kept it in my spirit and would not let go. Finally, I heard what Norvel Hayes was saying. A person must listen to something fifteen times before the message gets down into their heart. Most of us will never see the blessings of God unless we get the blessing we are grasping for solidified within our heart.

The next morning was the first day of the soon to be the best days of my life. At 8 a.m., I went out and stood in front of my work van, stretched forth my right hand and began to bless my business. The right hand symbolically represents the faith and blessings of God's pleasures forevermore (Psalms 16:11; Matthew 25:33).

I blessed my work van day after day, week after week, for over two months because it represented my business. Various neighbors noticed me walking around my van with my Bible open quoting scripture and blessing it. I called in business from the North, South, East and West. I knew promotion came from God, who is the judge of all the earth: He puts down one, and sets up another (Psalms 75:6-7). I was making prophetic declarations by calling in work form these four specific directions every day. The words of my mouth and the meditation of my heart had become acceptable in the sight of God.

The **North** symbolically speaks of the place of God's throne, the mount of the congregation on the farthest sides of the north (Isaiah 14:13). I would decree something aloud such as this, "The Lord God has declared I am innocent by the blood of Jesus Christ His Son. I have the divine favor of the Godhead as a shield and a canopy over my life. My business will live and not die; it will prosper and abound in the blessings and divine favor of God."

The **South** symbolically speaks of the place where we will receive refreshment from the hand of God. It is in the South where the Lord will open the streams of refreshing (Psalms 126:4).

I would call forth the blessings of refreshing and restoration that the Lord God has declared that I would walk in and no demon in hell will stop His decree from coming forth with fruit. I would call in fresh new accounts by the grace of God.

The **East** symbolically speaks of the place of the rising of the glory of God. Behold the glory of the God of Israel came from the way of the east. His voice was like the sound of many waters; and the earth shone with His glory (Ezekiel 43:1-2).

I would call for new work and new customers. I commanded and demanded that new blessings would come forth and flood my spirit, soul, body and my bank account. I declared that day was a blessed day because the Son of God had risen with healing in His wings and He had healed my business, giving me the best jobs—the gravy jobs—for the Lord God has blessed me in the natural and in the spiritual.

A person may not have a natural bank account. However, I do know this: we all have a spiritual bank account. We know what a natural bank account is. I compare a spiritual bank account with our natural bank account. In the natural, we make deposits of money into a bank account. When we have money in that account we may write a check for that amount making withdrawals.

The way you make deposits into your heavenly bank account is through the Matthew 6 principle. The **First Cord** that God the Holy Spirit revealed to me gives us an outline for our giving. Notice I did not say tithe! The tithe is what we owe. The tithe is a command of ten percent. In my household, we pay a tithe of ten percent of the gross income, not from the net income. If you need freedom in your finances, you had better get into giving offerings. It is in the giving of an offering that commands the blessings of God to overtake us. The offering is over and above our tithe. If all you are going to do is give your tithe, God will bless you. But, if you want the greater blessings to overtake you, then you will have to do something greater than just giving a tithe. You will never change what you believe until your belief does not produce what you desire. When you want something that you have never had, you will have to do something you have never done.

There are three immutable New Testament laws involving the giving of offerings I consider each time before I give an offering. I know when I give I will receive it all back in a greater measure (Luke 6:38). Lying spirits will not deceive me, for I will not mock God: whatever I sow, that will I also reap (Galatians 6:7-8). Because I choose to reap bountifully, I refuse to sow sparingly. I will enter into the grace of God and His abundance for my good work (2 Corinthians 9:6-10). These three irreversible, laws will always correctly point me to my spiritual compass, which is Jesus. He is the author and finisher of our faith (Hebrews 12:2).

The **Second Cord** is in (Matthew 6:5-7) which specifically speaks of praying in secret—that is without others knowing what we are petitioning God for. Do not go around telling everyone what you are asking God to do in your life. I do my best to follow the guidelines the apostle Paul laid down. I rejoice always, pray without ceasing, and in everything give thanks I do not quench the Spirit. Do not despise prophecies. Test all things; hold fast what is good. Abstain from every form of evil (1 Thessalonians 5:16-22).

In addition, the **Third Cord** is in Matthew 6:16-18. This powerful revelation concerns fasting. Fasting ties the knot in the threefold cord. It was the crowning of the first two. This is what gave power to our giving and our prayers. This cord does the binding to make sure it is strong and will not break under any attack by the evil one. Fasting has an interesting empowerment. If we want to receive from the Lord, we must prepare to receive His blessings. No one puts New Wine into old wineskins; or else the New Wine will burst the wineskins, and both the wine and the wineskins ruined. Nevertheless, New Wine goes into new wineskins, and both are preserved (Mark 2:22; Luke 5:37-38).

Fasting actually prepares us for the New Wine of our time. If you want to go far beyond where you are spiritually, my friend, begin to do a little fasting. For an example, if I am going to do a three day fast, I determine when I will began and where I will do the fast. To fast three full days means I will miss three meals a day for three days. The average meal out cost approximately three dollars that equates to nine dollars a day or twenty seven dollars over the period of those three days.

Next, I determine who I will send a twenty seven dollar offering to. Normally I send my offering to a ministry that feeds the poor and homeless, then I pray, pray, pray. Fasting without prayer is just another form of dieting. Fasting without giving is not following the directions Jesus gave us. During my fast, I read scripture and wait on the Lord to give me understanding and clarity of vision as to what I am fasting for. I make a list with pen and pad. I try to spend equal time in waiting before the Lord as I do in prayer and reading my Bible. I drink only water during the days I am fasting—I normally fast three days.

I personally believe when Jesus gave us the teaching on giving, praying and fasting, He gave us three stepping stones to follow to obtain our desired results. These three stepping stones reveal His grace, mercy and compassion and are very similar to a spiritual road map; follow them and we can go anywhere. Each of the three stones contains a different degree of authority and power (Mark 4:8).

The **West** symbolically speaks of the place of the sunset: an ending of that time; so shall they fear the name of the Lord from the west, and His glory from the rising of the sun (Isaiah 59:19). "Many will come from east and west, and sit down with Abraham, Isaac, and Jacob in the kingdom of heaven" (Matthew 8:11).

At times I would shake my fist in the air at the devil and declare its over, it is finished. I win, devil you lose. God is for me so who can be against me. All my bills are paid I owe no one and I have plenty of money in my bank account. So keep your hands off my money, my business, my van and my family.

After my neighbors observed me standing in front of my work van with my Bible open and quoting scripture for several weeks they became a little worried. One neighbor came over and asked me what I was doing. After I explained, I was labeled a spiritual nut. This same neighbor felt that it was his responsibility to warn all my other neighbors to stay away from me.

Some days I would slap the side of my van and say, "Van! You will have plenty of work you will not break down and you will get exceptional gas mileage. You will live and not die says the Lord God." The Bible did not say

I would have what Jesus says about my situation. The Bible did not say that I would have what someone else says about my situation. The Bible says, "**I will have what I say about my situation.**" That statement means my spirit, soul, and body must line up and obey what I say. Whatever words come out of my mouth my body must comply too.

Lastly, in addressing the West saying, "I have abundance and I will sit down and rest from all my labors. I have overcome all things and I am victorious, Amen. Thank You, Lord Jesus. It is over, I win." As a man thinks in their heart so is he! As I had said earlier, I kept doing this for several months. Eventually the windows of heaven opened over me (Malachi 3:10).

Open Heavens

Thursday morning began as usual. This was the third month without work. I had been out to my work van and did my daily confession. Once again, I was preparing to go hand out business cards, flyers, and knock on doors this is actively waiting on God. As I opened the door to leave, my phone rang. What a great sound that was! Although I quickly answered it, I kept my conversation cool. The person on the other end of the phone asked if I could meet him at a well known hotel at 2 p.m. that afternoon to look at a plumbing job. I quickly checked my schedule and assured him I would make time to meet.

As I drove over to the meeting, I wondered why he chose to call my company. The meeting totally blew me away. He wanted my company to handle a major plumbing remodeling job. At the time, I was my only employee. The supervisor informed me to have my crews at the job site by 9 a.m. Saturday morning to begin the work. He suggested I bring with me no less than twenty employees. For a minute or so, the request almost over whelmed me. He asked one question, "Can you do this job?" Without even giving it a second thought, I heard one word come out of my spirit man "YES."

On my way back to my home office, I asked God where I was going to find 20 plumbers. To my surprise, I heard in the Holy Spirit say, "He did not ask for twenty plumbers; he asked for twenty men." A measure of peace and grace came with that statement from the Lord. As soon as I arrived back at the office, I began calling and hiring men who needed work.

Saturday morning I arrived at daylight just in case some employees showed up early. I was glad I did. Two men arrived at the same time I did. As it turned out, these two men became the best employees. At 9 a.m. I did a head count. 18 men out of twenty showed up. I had to admit. "Not bad at all."

For a team of drifters and nobodies, we all worked as if we had been flowing and going together in the plumbing field for decades. None of the eighteen missed a day of work the first week, nor did I have to let anyone go. As it turned out, each one of them, sixteen in all, came to me one at a time and told me they could not keep working. The job had begun to slow down and I only needed two full time men, and I had those two. My agreement was for labor only as the contractor furnished all materials. Four months later, my company had taken in over $84,000, and to my dismay, the job ended.

On the day the job came to an end, I paused and asked the contractor who hired me why he had chosen my company. He smiled and said "Do you not know? Or are you just joking?" Then he told me that the president of this major international hotel chain in California had found one of my plumbing cards in his top desk drawer and told the Tennessee construction firm to use my plumbing company exclusively, "No matter what it cost." That business card must have had the fingerprints of God all over it.

The Shekinah Glory

Several months later, the economy was back to normal and I realized I was going to have some slow time between jobs. I called around and checked out some ads in a Christian magazine. I found out Christian International was hosting an "Apostles and Prophets Conference" in Pensacola, Florida during my slow time. I booked two places at the conference for my pastor and me along with hotel and air travel. This turned out to be a trial and a test for me. I am not sure I passed the entire test, but the Lord knew my heart.

After arriving, we settled into our hotel room and began the first session of the conference. The second night of the conference I dreamed my return ticket was lost.

When I woke up, I began looking for it and could not find it anywhere. This is where I felt I had missed the mark. I panicked, I did not have enough money, nor did I have a credit card, to purchase another airline ticket home. I tore our hotel room up from top to bottom. We even went out to the airport during the afternoon break to see if they had kept it at the ticket desk where we lingered while waiting for our rental car. I could not find the ticket anywhere. We went back to the conference for the evening service. The entire time, I kept seeing a vision of my suitcase in my mind and did not know why. Later that night, when we returned to our hotel room, I looked through my suitcase again. As I was placing the suitcase back on the floor, I noticed an outside compartment I thought I had not used or checked before. I reached in the compartment and felt nothing. As I pulled my hand out, I heard the Holy Spirit say, "reach in again," so I did. This time when I pulled out my hand, I was holding my return ticket. The moment I looked at the ticket, I had a vision. In the vision, I saw the ticket agent place my ticket into the compartment and place a destination band on the handle before giving the suitcase back to me as a carryon.

    I was somewhat embarrassed. Here I am at a Prophets and Apostles conference, with my pastor, and I could not hear God about where my ticket was. It seemed to amuse my pastor, and it took some time before I lived that incident down.

The last night of the conference, about 2000 people were present when Bishop Hamon asked all the Apostles and Prophets to stand. I stood to my feet and motioned for my pastor to stand also.

He said, "I am not a prophet or an apostle".

To that statement, I informed him he was wrong and that he had the call of an apostle on him before birth (Jeremiah 1:5). Although I told him that, he remained seated.

I stood along with approximately 450 others. Bishop Hamon then invited the Holy Spirit to come and anoint everyone standing. As I stood with both hands lifted up, I felt a heavy thick dew or fog descend into the auditorium and over my body. Although the dew felt damp (similar to fog), it was not sopping wet and it did not fall past my chest. I said, God what is this that is happening. At that very moment, my spiritual eyes opened and I saw what looked like a bright yellow fog had filled the entire room. The dew or fog remained about four feet above the floor and extended all the way up to the ceiling. I asked, "Is this scriptural?" I heard the Lord say, "My teachings are as drops of rain and my speech as distilled dew" (Deuteronomy 32:2).

A person cannot be in the presence of the Shekinah Glory without the Glory of God affecting your spirit, soul and body in a greater way. Illumination came to my spiritual eyes that day revealing the greater things of God. My spirit and soul entered into a realm of the supernatural that was refreshing and peaceful. My body remained the same but it was as if I had a glow all over me for a few minutes after encountering the Shekinah Glory (Exodus 34:29). The word, will and ways of God began coming forth with greater clarity from that time on. After I encountered the Shekinah Glory, my life became very different from that day forth. As it turned out, 1991 became a spiritually unique new beginning for me.

Faith to Receive the Supernatural

I developed a habit of asking for an opportunity to be in the same prophetic meeting with Mr. Cain. I prayed that request so long that my faith had grown to a new level. I was surprised the day I heard myself say, "Father God, You are not a respecter of persons and I believe, if Brother Paul would only call out my name, you will anoint me with a very similar anointing!"

I kept seeking God with all my heart. I would often lose track of time and found myself lost in scripture. I would sit for hours and copy scripture into a spiral notebook. I knew if I would do what I could God would do what I could not do. The angel told Peter to put on his shoes and garment, which he was able to do, but it was not in Peter's ability to lose his chains or open the Iron Gate. Peter did what he was capable of doing and God sent an angel to do what Peter could not (Acts 12).

I wanted the Bible in my spirit so that I could call up scripture in a moment. At one point, I had over fifty spiral notebooks full of hand written scripture. I do not really know why I chose to do such a thing, but once I began to write scripture, it became natural for me. To this day at times, I will lose myself in copying scripture just to free my mind from everyday life. I may write the same verse repeatedly or a chapter or an entire book. Once I made it a goal to write the Psalms and the book of Proverbs, which turned out to be a very time consuming venture.

Answered prayer came in March of 1991. I attended a Vineyard prophetic conference in Arlington, Texas. I met John Wimber, and saw the mantle of wisdom and humility that was upon him. When I shook his hand I could smell the fragrance of ants come into the room! On the first night of the conference, Lenard Ravenhill called forth the spirit of repentance. By the end of the evening, everyone present had his or her face in the carpet sobbing. It was one of the greatest supernatural blessings I have ever experienced in a prophetic gathering.

The next night, Brother Paul preached and cancelled the spirit of depression over the entire audience. Later that night in my hotel room, I felt something in my stomach break. The very moment that occurred, in my mind I saw a stick that had snapped in half. All at once, I began laughing uncontrollably. That night I did not sleep. I laughed all night long and most of the next day. I felt tired and worn out, yet at the same time, I was excited and felt powerful in my spirit man. At times it felt as if electricity was flowing through my entire body. The electricity reminded me of the first year of my salvation when the electricity flowed through my mind every time I read the word of God. Somehow, I managed to make it back to the conference the next day, and I am so glad I did.

On the third night of the conference as the Vineyard worship team led us in worship, I entered into the greatest praise and worship I have ever encountered in my life. That evening, I sat in an aisle seat in front of the pulpit. Brother Paul instructed everyone who was in ministry to stand to his or her feet. He announced that the angels of God were present and they were walking up and down the aisles anointing everyone standing. These angels were imparting gifts, callings and divine favor from God the Father.

As I stood with both hands lifted high, an angel passed by and slapped the backside of my right hand. The moment he did so, I saw in my mind the backside of my hand as black as if a dark shade had come over it. The Lord is my keeper; The Lord is the shade on your right hand (Psalm 121:5). To this day, at times this black or dark shade appears in the spirit realm. Each time it occurs, the backside of that hand feels like electricity flowing through it; that is when I know God is up to something therefore, I just lay hands on people and bless them in the name of the Lord Jesus.

I have learned over the years that when the shade is present on my hand and I lay hands on anyone, they will experience an electrifying touch from God. Some have received healing while others have been set free of physical addictions.

On the last night of the conference, I tried to get a closer seat to the platform to hear Brother Paul preach the closing message. To my dismay the closest seat available was twenty rows back from the platform.

Another discouraging thing came right after I sat down. I was told Brother Paul would not be doing any prophetic call outs for the rest of the conference. Though disappointed, I enjoyed the teaching and I was very surprised that after Brother Paul had closing prayer, he said, "Duane Young–stand to your feet." During the entire time he prophesied, I felt a rushing, warm, wind blowing all over my body. The warm wind was so strong my hair and my shirt were fluttering.

During that last day of the conference, Psalm 121 kept coming to my mind. I had a strong impression that Psalms 121 was for Brother Paul, but I had no way of telling him. After the conference was over, as I was walking out of the building, I heard someone call my name and say, "Duane your personal Psalm is Psalm 121." I stopped and looked back to see who was talking. I saw no one I knew or anyone who would have known me. I asked a couple who were walking past me if they saw who it was that called out my name saying Psalm 121 was my Psalm. They assured me no one had said a word. They gave me a strange look and quickly walked away.

On the way back home, the couple I was riding with stopped to get fuel and soft drinks. I noticed that my soft drink had printed on its lid in bright yellow letters, "Look inside for prize." I quickly unscrewed the bottle cap and saw the number "121" with the word "WINNER" in red capital letters. Later that day, I began to notice Word of Knowledge, Wisdom and Prophecy began flowing through me when I least expected it. Although I was really enjoying this new blessing, I was also concerned.

What did this mean and why was it happening to me? Then I remembered my prayer several months before I had made a request unto the Lord for such a gifting.

The day I arrived home my youngest daughter also arrived home from a field trip. She had purchased a small New Testament Bible in a little silver case for me. The Bible was only 1 inch tall, ¾ inches wide and ½ inch thick. As she handed me the little Bible, she jokingly said, "Daddy, don't you wish you could just swallow this little silver Bible and know everything that's in it?" Graciously, I accepted my daughter's gift and smiled thinking that would be nice.

That evening as I was having my devotional time, I began to think back at what my daughter had said concerning eating the little Bible. I thought back to my first year as a believer and all the times in prayer I would ask God if there were any way He could somehow open up my mind and put His word into me. As I pondered that foolish idea, I smiled and said aloud, "Only believe, Duane; if you would only believe all things are possible."

Although my plans were to relax during that Easter eve, I had a mountain of unanswered mail and had to finish some much needed paper work. In addition it seemed everyone I had ever worked for needed a return call. On top of all this, I was winding down from the gruesome schedule of going and coming from a prophetic conference. I had always heard how physically exhausting conferences were on people and now I had to agree with that statement.

I needed to fax a "Thank You" letter along with a prayer request to Brother Paul. I had obtained his fax number and that was the only item on my list I really wanted to concentrate on that day. I stopped by a friend's house and as I was pulling out of their driveway, heading to the fax center, I had an "Open vision." An open vision is like watching a huge television screen. In the vision, I saw Brother Paul holding a pair of brown (brown speaks of humility) wingtip shoes. He looked straight at me and never said a word. Immediately I heard the Holy Spirit say, "Duane, he is sending those shoes to you."

I began to wonder, how he knew my shoe size and where I lived. When I arrived back home, I informed my children I was expecting a package later that week and to accept the package because Brother Paul was sending me a pair of shoes.

It was 8 p.m. before I sat down at my kitchen table to have a cup of coffee and read my Bible. I began to think about the open vision, when I was surprised. Suddenly, all the air in the kitchen and dining area felt like electricity was flowing through it. As I was trying to figure out what was happening, the Holy Spirit overtook me and I was slain in the spirit I slumped forward in my chair as I sat at my kitchen table. The next thing I became aware of was the presence of an angel standing to my right side. I had no strength to even lift or turn my head. I tried, but I could not move my eyeballs.

The angel placed one hand on my chest and lifted me back into an upright position in my chair. Next, he lifted my chin, tilting my head to the backwards position.

Then he gently pulled my jaw down and opened my mouth. I could feel him placing a thick sweet substance in my mouth. The substance resembled honey in its thickness and its taste. In fact, it tasted much sweeter than any honey I had ever tasted.

"I opened my mouth, and he caused me to eat, and to fill my belly with the sweet substance. I ate it and it was in my mouth as honey for sweetness. How sweet are the words of the Lord to my taste, Sweeter than honey to my mouth" (Ezekiel 3:1-3; Psalm 119:103).

I began having a second open vision, which lasted 45 minutes. I saw a wheel spinning clockwise with seven bright white lights, which looked like seven flames of fire. In the center of the wheel, was the face of a man with ocean blue eyes; he was smiling at me. Although I felt as if he was looking through me, I felt peace and love flowing from Him into me. I was unable to hide my feelings or thoughts.

"I saw the face of a man, and the wheel upon the earth by the living creatures, with his four faces" (Ezekiel 1:10, 15).

Five years later the Prophet Bob Jones told me that the man I saw in the wheel was the Lord Jesus.

During the next 45 minutes, I had seven separate visions. All seven visions related to the universal Church specifically to the end times. For we know in part and we prophesy in part but when the perfect comes, there will be no more partial (1 Corinthians 13:9-10). I do not reveal all seven visions in this book. I do however expound on each one when I speak at meetings.

The Lord revealed many would have their life extended beyond their allotted time, allowing them to fulfill their work for the Kingdom of God. Many would live to see three generations of children come into the supernatural things of God. This is a portion of Joel's prophecy (Joel 1:3). We will tell our children of God's grace, mercy and compassion, and let our children tell their children, and their children tell another generation.

Many would live an extra ten, fifteen or even twenty years. A few would have an additional thirty years added to their life. This group would live longer than anyone else in his or her family linage (Proverbs 3:1, 2; 9:11).

I saw "The Faceless Generation" performing signs, wonders and miracles. I have good news for you all. The faceless generation is not just going to be the young. A vast majority of the faceless generation would also include the middle aged and older people as well. These individuals would be no less anointed than the young people will. During this time, everyone will function with child like faith. Whoever does not receive the kingdom of God as a little child will by no means enter it (Mark 10:15).

While this was occurring, I was still chewing the sweet honey like substance the angel had placed in my mouth. Swallowing this sweet honey like substance was extremely difficult. This sweet honey was thicker and sweeter than any honey I had ever eaten. Nine months later, my stomach became bitter (Revelation 10:9-10). The seven things which were shown to me will help usher in the return of the Lord Jesus Christ.

These end times miracles would begin as a local movement, expand to a statewide movement that would grow into a nationwide movement within a few weeks, and then grow into a worldwide movement. This faceless generation was leading countless numbers into salvation, creative miracles and healing were abounding everywhere you looked. Everyone was operating in the last days' signs and wonders, which is the last alter call given on planet earth.

"And the Spirit and the bride say, "Come!" "And let him who hears say, "Come!" "And let him who thirsts come. And whoever desires let him take the water of life freely" (Revelation 22:17).

This last great outpouring of the Spirit of Grace would release a supernatural opportunity for the lost, hungry, hurting and dying souls. The number of those receiving salvation would surpass all of the moves of the Holy Spirits outpourings of old. Billions of people would give their hearts to the Lord Jesus Christ. Billions of people would become sons and daughters of the Most High God and Savior. Billions of people would receive the baptism of the Holy Spirit of promise. Billions of people would begin a new journey of joy unspeakable.

"Whom having not seen, ye love; in whom, though now ye see him not, yet believing, ye rejoice with joy unspeakable and full of glory: Receiving the end of your faith, even the salvation of your souls" (1 Peter 1:8-9).

All of this was happening just by the laying on of hands, which consisted mainly of children (not necessarily young in age but children in Christ; many had only been Christians for a short time). Prophetic words with a supernatural level of authority and power that brought forth life from the dead; Aaron's rod had blossomed (Numbers 17:8). This faceless generation has authority and power over "ALL" the diseases of this world. It is important to understand that this group has both authority and power. Authority without power is futile, and power without authority is futile. The blessing of the early rain and the latter rain coming together released a beautiful fragrance and the most peaceful experience I had ever had seen or heard. The sweet fragrance of blessing that filled the air went beyond the boundaries of the stadiums and sports arenas. The fragrance of blessing was very similar to what fills the air after a heavy rainstorm purifying and cleaning the air. These winds of fragrances of blessings contained a joy unspeakable and became a drawing card. God in these last hours has truly saved the best wine for last (John 2:10). He has prepared something for us that we will not have room enough to contain. We will go out into the highways and byways, and give this blessing away to the hurting, the homeless, the lost, widows and orphans, and to anyone and everyone (Luke 14:23).

While I was slain in the spirit, the angel standing next to me said, "You have been given a realm of authority and power over all forms of cancer" (cancer is any form of disease that destroys the human body). Had I not been in the condition I was, I would have jumped up and ran out the door at that statement but not in joy.

The death of my neighbor had always plagued my memory. Instead of eating lunch, I stopped by the hospital to pray for his healing. This was the first time I had prayed for anyone with cancer after becoming a radical believer. I just knew God was going to heal him. He died one hour after I left the hospital. I was devastated. I did not understand why God did not heal him. From that day forward, I would not pray for anyone who had of a fatal disease.

As the angel stood next to me, he said, "And the Spirit and the bride say, "Come!" "And let him who hears say, "Come!" "And let him who thirsts come. Whoever desires let him take the water of life freely'" (Revelation 22:17). This will be the last great alter call on earth.

Finally, I somehow managed to swallow the last of the thick substance that tasted sweeter than honey and the visions stopped (Ezekiel 3:1-3; Revelation 10:9-11). I remained sitting in my chair for well over an hour, slumped back and just looking at my kitchen ceiling. The entire time I wondered what had happened? I did not feel any fear I was totally puzzled and shocked about what just happened. It was 10 p.m. before I regained enough physical strength to set up in my chair. Finally, I managed to get up and wash my face. I stood at the sink and washed my face several times more but nothing changed. I was still in my kitchen and had some kind of an encounter with God and a heavenly being from the throne room of heaven.

    I went over and sat back down at my kitchen table trying to gather my thoughts when all of a sudden, the room felt like electricity again and I began having another open vision. This time I was seeing the inside of the church I was attending. I knew it was Easter morning service, and the entire church was jammed packed—mainly with visitors. I was looking at the faces of two people I had never seen before. One was a single man, and the other was a married woman. I knew neither of them knew the other and the one thing they had in common was that neither of them knew Jesus Christ. I realized this would be the last Easter service they would ever attend. I heard their names and the names of a close relative who had been praying for them. This came by revelation. I knew there would be three people in the service that morning diagnosed with a fatal disease. This particular open vision lasted for nearly twenty minutes.

    After the vision lifted, I remained seated. I was totally worn out, mentally and a physically tired and on a spiritual high all at the same time. This time it took me even longer to regain enough strength to get up from my chair. At midnight I decided to lay down although I knew in my spirit there was no way that I would ever go to sleep. I went to bed and as I was lying there, it seemed as if my mind was racing a hundred miles an hour. I laid on my bed as I tried to figure out all I had encountered during the past four hours.

While I was lying there, I began to become extremely hot. I became so hot I thought I was going to have a heat stroke. I kicked my feet out from under the covers and the next thing I knew, the air in the bedroom felt like electricity. I felt the presence of the angel again. This time he was standing at the foot of my bed, yet I saw no one. By now, I had become worried. What was happening to me? Was I going out of my mind? I was not fearful, but I was extremely concerned with everything that had already occurred. I was extremely weak, unable to move a finger, and slain in the spirit. The shoes did arrive, but not by UPS, Fed Ex or by U.S mail; they arrived by an angel.

The angel picked up my right foot and placed a shoe on it. Then he picked up my left foot and placed a shoe on it. Next, I could feel him lace up the right shoe and then the left shoe. It was at that very moment I realized these were the same shoes I had seen the man of God sending me earlier that day. The shoes came by angelic delivery in the spiritual realm. These were spiritual shoes. They were the shoes of the gospel of peace. I had prayed for these shoes for over three years so that my feet would be shod with the preparation of the gospel of peace (Ephesians 6:15).

When the experience was finished, my strength immediately returned and I was able to stand to my feet. I jumped out of bed and these words came out of my mouth before I realized it "They are a little tight, but they will do just fine, thank you Lord Jesus, Amen." I spent the rest of the night drinking coffee, reading my Bible and praying.

By daylight all that had happened to me kept washing through my spirit man. I finally realized I had just begun my spiritual journey and eternal quest. My commissioning was not only life-changing, but something I would never forget. Little did I realize that it would take all the faith I could muster up and a huge amount of patience to enter into all the Lord God had put within me. I began to see that I had entered into a greater and higher level of the prophetic than I had ever experienced in my walk with God. What was so troubling to me was I did not know what to do with everything I had encountered this past week. I began to feel that I was less qualified than ever before. My daily prayer was and still is, "Oh God Please Help."

As usual Easter Sunday I arrived at church early and went to the prayer room to enter into the presence of the Lord. As I sat praying, I began to feel as if my body was growing up and out through the ceiling of the prayer room. Fear swept through me, I stopped praying, and the experience stopped. During these past years, I regretted becoming fearful on that day. I wish I had allowed the Lord to do as He desired. I still pray that God will give me another opportunity to enter into this spiritual occurrence.

As the congregation sang some of those beautiful old gospel hymns, I could not keep from looking around trying to spot the faces I had seen the night before in the open vision. I did not recognize anyone I had seen in the vision. Finally, I decided I needed a better view so I approached my pastor who graciously allowed me to address the congregation. The moment I look up, I saw the two individuals. The woman was sitting on the second pew and the man was sitting on the third pew both directly in front of the podium. I declared what the Holy Spirit had revealed to me the prior evening. It was easy to see that both were squirming in their seats. Neither responded when a special alter call was given. Because there was no response to the alter call for salvation, I sure did not want to risk calling out cancer, so I stopped, left the sanctuary, and went to the prayer room to pray.

I went and hid in the prayer room—that is exactly what I did; I went and hid because I felt I had failed God. I prayed and cried out for me and for everyone in the main sanctuary. I began to feel a lifting in my spirit man. I began to feel like everything would be ok. Later several individuals did respond to the pastor's altar call. By the grace of God, there were two rededications and two others—one man and one woman came forth for salvation. I never disclosed to the pastor who the two were, but I believe the Lord managed to get the message across to them.

After the Easter morning service, several couples went out to a local restaurant. Upon arriving at the restaurant, I immediately came under attack. My eyes began to burn and pain swept through my body. Everywhere I looked, I saw people and knew their unrepented sins. It was bad...so bad I could not stay, I excused myself from lunch and went home to hide and pray.

Later that evening I went to a local mall to pick up a catalog order. While waiting for a sales clerk the spirit of compassion flooded my spirit. Everywhere I looked, I saw sheep without a shepherd. After I arrived at home, I called my pastor and said, "Quick! Get over to the mall there are thousands of unsaved people walking around shopping." "That's good Duane, you just win them all to Jesus ok, goodbye see you tomorrow." Do not take this wrong my pastor is a loving man and wants everyone to receive Jesus as his or her savior. However, my declaration was a little more than he was accustomed to.

I became aware as I read scripture that I had begun to see things I had never known or had never seen before. I came to the realization the honey I had been feed opened my spiritual eyes just as it did Jonathan when he put forth the end of the rod in his hand, dipped it in a honeycomb, and put his hand to his mouth; his eyes were enlightened (1 Samuel 14:27).

When I am not experiencing spiritual manifestations I need to draw aside and spend some quality time fasting and praying. The worst enemy for all Christians is the spirit of slothfulness. When we become lukewarm and complacent, the Lord will not answer our prayers (Revelation 3:16-22).

Poland: An open vision in 1994

In this encounter, the Lord took me into the heavens and we went to Poland. Upon arriving in Poland I found myself standing on a public street, I saw an old man walking beside a horse pulling a wooden wagon filled with brown straw. As I watched them, I noticed the man's continence became more joyful with every step he took. In addition, the horse began to get friskier with ever step. Even the straw began to change its color from a dingy brown to a soft yellow color. That is when I noticed pages from the Bible were covering every street, sidewalk or walkway in the nation of Poland. God will personally bombard Poland with His holy word. The day will come when every man and beast will walk and stand on the uncompromised word of God. In one day, the hearts of the people will change and the entire nation of Poland will become a Christian nation (Isaiah 65:1).

SECTION #3
1992

My wife had departed, and I found myself alone after many years of marriage. The old surroundings brought back all the fond memories of our many years together and I just could not handle that so I moved to big D just off of Diamond Town Road. To this day when I see any news broadcast concerning a person dying in an automobile fire I still remember my deceased wife.

The Apartment

It was September when I rented an apartment in the suburbs of "Big D." I had chosen an apartment based on its convenient location between the fellowship I was attending and my office.

The manager showed me a downstairs apartment that was unfit to live in. As she was unlocking the apartment's door, she said, "I have a newly remodeled upstairs apartment with this same square footage and floor plan that is clean and bug free. I am only showing you this apartment because I cannot leave the office very long and this one is the closest vacant apartment by my office. This will give you an idea of what we have to offer."

The downstairs apartment's bedroom floor was cracked and had weeds coming up through the crack. The crack was three inches wide making the room three inches lower on one side. I could spit faster than the water flowed from the plumbing fixtures. In every room, I could easily count twenty or more cockroaches two inches long or longer climbing up the walls or running across the floor.

I chuckled to myself as I turned to leave the dump. I told her I would take the upstairs apartment. Immediately I heard a voice say, "No, you take this one." I began commanding in Jesus name that spirit to leave. Finally the Holy Spirit said, "Be quiet and tell her you are going to take this apartment."

When I told her this, her mouth nearly hit the floor saying, "You are crazy! You cannot walk up a few stairs? You know I am going to have to charge you the same for either apartment, so why don't you go ahead and take the nice one?"

Finally, I convinced her I was hearing God, and this was where He wanted me to live—at least for a while. As I said those words in my spirit, I was hoping it would not be very long—maybe a month or less.

Moving day arrived and none of my help showed up so I moved by myself. As I was wrestling with a box springs and mattress, my new neighbor saw my struggle and came out to help me.

"I am Mr. Shivers," he said, as he reached out to shake my hand. His next sentence shocked me. "I do not believe in prophets or speaking in other tongues." I wondered why he said that. I thought to myself, "He may be a little prophetic and does not realize it. Boy, oh boy, you are in for a big surprise!"

"... Hear me, O Judah and you inhabitants of Jerusalem believe in the Lord your God. And you shall be established; believe His prophets, and you shall prosper" (2 Chronicles 20:20).

After I assembled my bed, remembering one side of my bedroom was three inches lower I found some bricks to make it almost level. The management had placed some used carpet in the bedroom, but when I pulled the carpet back, the three inch crack now had dead weeds sticking out from it. By the end of the first week in the new apartment, I noticed three young men who always sat on the sidewalk across from my apartment; they took turns reading from a big black book. Sometimes one or all of them would extend a hand towards my apartment and mumble something. They all wore black pants, black shirts, and had their hair dyed black. All three had a dragon tattoo on their left forearms and wore a skeleton head necklace that hung from black leather shoestrings down to their waist.

I recognized my neighbor's voice when he shouted, "Satan worshippers; that's who they are over there, just a bunch of Satan worshippers," as he pointed towards the apartment across from my door. "Every day when I came home from work those same young men are sitting across from my apartment reading out loud from that big, black, witch's book."

That particular day was a little different. They were all making gestures with their hands, and at times were cursing aloud. I did not know if they were trying to scare me by saying and doing that stuff, but it did not work. I knew they were doing their best to release fear, doubt and unbelief, not to mention evil. It appeared they were actually trying to do something for the devil. Looking up I saw Mr. Shivers and said, "God loves them also." When I made that statement, he shook his head from side to side saying, "I guess so," and quickly changed the subject.

I did not give those three young men a second thought but rather went on about my business. Within several days, Mr. Shivers and his wife had become my new friends. I learned Mr. and Mrs. Shivers had grown up in the same denomination and met at the same East Texas Church. Mr. Shivers made sure I knew he was more into his church's beliefs and traditions than his wife and was very proud of that.

Every evening, I would sit at my kitchen table, drink coffee, pray, read scripture and throw beanbags. My right shoulder muscle had become tender and sore from throwing beanbags at the cockroaches that were crawling up my walls all the time. I had a pellet pistol, but could not find it or I would have shot the huge critters. My first night in the apartment was horrible. I spent most of the night swatting roaches from my face. So far the roaches were winning—but not for long. I had called a friend who owned an exterminating company. I made an agreement with him to trade plumbing labor for exterminating labor. He was coming by to kill "ALL" those huge critters. Each morning at 6 a.m., I would turn on the bath water in the tub before leaving for work. By 8 p.m., the tub would have about five inches of water in it, and I would take a bath in cold water since I did not have hot water in my apartment at all. Sometimes, I would scoop out several gallons of cold tub water and heat it on my kitchen stove. This warmed the water up to an "eye opening temperature." I purchased bottled water to drink and make coffee. That left me with only one other water problem—dishwashing. I finally came up with the idea of leaving my sink water running from midnight when I went to bed until I turned if off at 6 a.m. By morning the water was deep enough to wash the dishes. I then added a little bleach to the cold water to obtain some level of sterilization for my dishes Dawn liquid and Clorox bleach: what a combination for dishwashing. The grease would break down but the soapiness remained. By the second week I realized I needed to heat that water on the stove also. It was nearly an all day job just preparing to wash dishes. I finally gave up, bought paper plates and cups, and threw everything away. Thank God, no more dishwashing.

    I quickly found myself beginning to doubt I heard God say move into this apartment. I began praying more than my normal amount of time, partially from my own misery. I found myself crying out daily. I began examining my past, looking for any kind of unconfessed sin that might have become a wedge between my heavenly Father and me. I was certain that my prayers were coming before His throne and He was hearing my entire request with an affirmation of "Yes, go for it." This began to puzzle me. If God was for me, why then did He want me to live in this place? Finally, late into the night, I heard the Holy Spirit say, "Be at peace my son all is well." With that, I became so greatly encouraged I did not care what the enemy threw at me.

Every evening Mr. and Mrs. Shivers would come over to visit for a short while. The first words out of his mouth were always, "Do you have any supper leftovers that need to be eaten?" Mrs. Shivers would always just drink coffee and want to talk about the infilling of the Holy Spirit. I always offered to lay hands on her to receive an impartation of the Holy Spirit, but her husband would insist they had to leave. I really felt sorry for her; she was four months pregnant with their first child and was the sole provider for their household.

One night I stayed up late making a huge pot of angel hair pasta and homemade spaghetti sauce with spicy Italian sausage, hoping that it would last me all week. Cooking was always a chore with the water problem. The following day was a laborious one, and I was glad to head back to my apartment. My mind quickly forgot all the trials of the day when I remembered that huge pot of angel hair pasta.

As I walked passed my neighbor's apartment, Mr. Shivers stuck his head out from his door and said, "Hey we are all coming over to your apartment for supper tonight. I took the liberty of crawling in your window after prying the locked screen open and saw that huge pot of pasta in your refrigerator." I could not believe what I was hearing. He went on to say, "Oh, and by the way, I invited those three Satan worshippers to supper also," he chuckled. "We all will be over in about an hour. Ok?"

I paused to look at my window and sure enough it had been broken into. The angel hair pasta, homemade spaghetti sauce with spicy Italian sausage was already simmering on the stove. I was standing in my kitchen in total disbelief when my living room door opened and in walked Mrs. Shivers.

The first words out of her mouth were, "Please forgive my husband." With tears in her eyes, she went on to explain how her husband was determined to rock my boat. He did not believe anything that did not come from his denominational beliefs and teachings. She did say, "I will tell you the truth, this is the first hot meal I will have eaten in over a week. It will be two more days before I am paid."

When she said those words, my cold, angry heart melted. Under my breath I said, "Lord God, please forgive me for judging your people, I am guilty, please be merciful to me, in Jesus name. Amen." I told her she would never go without food or a hot meal from that day forth. I assured her my front door would be unlocked, and she could help herself to any food in my apartment and refrigerator. I found out some of the foods she liked and made sure I had those on hand from that day on.

Seven o'clock came rather fast. I barely had enough time to take a quick, cold bath. You would be surprised how quickly you can bathe when the water is cold. I hurriedly dressed and rounded the corner of my living room just as the satan worshippers walked through my front door. I introduced myself and motioned for them to have a chair at my kitchen table with Mr. and Mrs. Shivers.

I took my seat at the head of the table and said, "If you eat at my table you will enter into a time of thanksgiving and prayer." I extended my hands towards two of the young men seated on each side of me. When the six of us had joined hands, I said, "Lord God, I ask for God the Holy Spirit to pour out His merciful grace upon my dinner guest and to have thy own way in Jesus name, Amen."

I did not release either of the satan worshipers' hands. I gently held each hand as a mother would hold the hand of her child. In a few seconds, both young men began shaking, trembling, and exhibiting a look of deep concern on their face. I glanced across the table towards the third satan worshiper and saw tears streaming down his cheeks. I said, "All three of you repeat these words out loud. Heavenly Father, please forgive me of all my sins. I ask Your Son, Jesus Christ, to come into my heart to live and guide me for the rest of my life. I freely give you my spirit, soul and body. I confess with my mouth that Jesus is Lord, and I believe in my heart God raised Him from the dead; therefore I will be saved. For with my heart I believe unto righteousness, and with my mouth, I confess You as Lord and Savior unto salvation. I ask this in Jesus name; Amen."

After saying this, you could have heard a pin drop. One by one the young men opened up and told his story at my supper table. That evening they all renounced the worship of Satan and received the Holy Spirit of promise. As children all three had attended a spirit filled church with their Christian parents. The boys had grown up as neighbors and friends but had gotten off track and into some deep sin. Before the evening was over, all three had washed their faces clean by the tears of joy and refreshing that can only come from the presence of the Lord God.

I did not want to miss a single opportunity, so when Mr. Shivers left to get Parmesan cheese from his apartment, I quickly laid hands on Mrs. Shivers and she also received the baptism of the Holy Spirit. She became drunk in the Spirit, full of joy and laughter. When her husband returned he was not sure what to make of all that was going on. He insisted they eat fast and return to their apartment for a time of prayer and solitude with God.

Saturday morning I heard a lot of door banging going on so I looked outside. I saw the three young men carrying furniture and boxes out to the carport. One stopped what he was doing and put down a box and said, "Mr. Young, you would not guess what we are doing.

"Moving, I think."

"Well, yes sir, we threw away all the black arts stuff, and we are all moving back home to be with our own parents." I let them know that I was proud for them making the correct decision. I congratulated them and went on to work.

A month passed, and the Shivers continued to visit on a regular basis. We shared many meals together, but to my sadness, Mr. Shivers refused to believe anything that was not from his "hard shell, male chauvinistic Doctrine."

One Friday, as I passed the Shivers apartment, I could hear someone inside crying. I stopped and knocked on the door but no one came to answer it. I reached out, turned the doorknob, and found it unlocked. I carefully opened the door and saw Mrs. Shivers sitting in her rocking chair, slowly rocking back and forth all doubled over holding her stomach, moaning and crying at the same time.

When she saw that it was me, she motioned for me to come in and take a seat next to her. Finally, she was able to talk saying "My doctor determined that these excruciating pains are a sure indication that my unborn baby has died. Today they did three sonograms at three different locations, and each sonogram gave the same results. My baby is dead. My doctor gave me the first sonogram at his office. Two hours later, I received a second one at a woman's clinic. I received the last sonogram at the emergency room. They all said my baby was dead and all recommended an abortion; I objected and left. Mr. Shivers had just gotten a job and had not accompanied her to the doctor, and he had not gotten the report yet.

All weekend I bombarded heaven on behalf of the Shivers and their unborn baby. At times, it seemed my prayers did not get past the ceiling; at other times I sensed the presence of the Holy Spirit in the room with me in agreement. Yet, all day Saturday and Sunday there seemed to be no real answer to any of my prayers. I went over to check on her condition once or twice and each time her husband informed me he felt the best thing was for her to have a cesarean section, which she refused to do. Although she was in pain, she was faithful and remained standing on the word of God. All weekend she cried from the excruciating pain but stood her ground and did not give up.

I had already made plans to attend a prophetic conference in San Antonio, Texas on Monday. As I packed my suitcase at 7:00 a.m., Monday morning, I heard the Holy Spirit say, "Take the bottle of baby oil next door and give it to the Shivers. Tell them their child will live and not die. Tell her she will give birth to a healthy, beautiful, baby girl, and the baby will have flaming red hair." I stood there pondering what I had just heard. It takes faith to do something such as this; do you know how to spell this type of faith? You spell it "Risk," that is how. The entire time I kept asking myself did I really hear God, or was I just thinking that I heard him?

I opened my medicine cabinet and there was an unopened bottle of baby oil. As I left for my ride, I stopped next door and knocked. Mr. Shivers jerked the door open and with anger in his voice, asked. "What do you want?"

I handed the bottle of baby oil to Mr. Shivers and said, "This is a token of the power of God the Holy Spirit." I then looked past him and saw Mrs. Shivers seated on their living room couch doubled over, crying. I said, "Your child will live and not die for the Lord has commanded the blessing life forevermore (Psalms 133:3). You will have a beautiful baby girl with flaming red hair. She will be totally healthy all the days of her life." I then turned and walked away. With each step, I could hear Mr. Shivers yelling, "You are a fake; you are a fool, and God does not talk to people like that anymore."

After returning home from the conference on Wednesday, I was told her husband did not take her for a fourth sonogram until Tuesday. I understood she remained in pain until the minute the nurse applied the cold gel on her rock hard stomach to check for heart tones. Mrs. Shivers said, "The very moment the nurse placed the sonogram's receiver on my stomach the baby kicked and the pain immediately stopped." Praise God!

A year later, I invited the entire Shivers family to our wedding. At the reception, Mr. and Mrs. Shivers proudly showed off their baby girl. I probably shouldn't have said anything, but I did. Taking the baby into my arms I asked, "Hey, from whose side of your family did this flaming red hair come from?" At that question, Mr. Shivers took the child out of my arms, turned and left the room.

I did not intend to upset him. However, when the word of the Lord declared, "the child will live and not die;

the baby will be a healthy, beautiful baby girl with flaming red hair," he called me a false prophet.

Angelic Interventions

As I was lying down for the evening, I had a vision of one of my daughters severely injured in an automobile accident. Three times this vision occurred. Three times, I set up in bed and cancelled the plans of the enemy. Each time I spoke, it felt as if my words were fire (Jeremiah 5:14). For a moment, I think that I felt a little like the prophet Jeremiah did.

That next week, shortly before supper, I received a phone call informing me that my daughter had just been involved in a major auto accident. I quickly drove to the location to find her seated in the waiting room of a Fast Lube shop as she waited for the police. I thanked God that she was all right. I reassured her everything would be ok, the car was replaceable she was not.

She then told me the story. A road raged driver in a pickup truck hit her head on. She had been waiting in the middle turn lane to flow into the traffic. Her car had been hit so hard it spun around three complete times, not hitting any other autos. When her car came to a stop, she looked to her left to see two male nurses in white uniforms. Both nurses had blond hair and gold badges on their chest with the initials "R.N." One nurse called my daughter by name, and told her that her dad was on his way. The second nurse had peeled the crushed car door back by hand. Later, I saw that the door had been rolled back as you would peel back the lid of a sardine can.

When the police arrived, they began to interview various individuals. My daughter told the officer that two male nurses in white uniforms carried her into the store. The people at the store said, "An old black man and woman carried her in." Another couple told the police an oriental man and woman carried her in. Everyone saw someone different. The police became upset with the conflicting reports and threatened to ticket everyone for obstruction of justice. Two angels had come to my daughter's rescue. Thank God!

To this day, she still has a difficult time realizing what a major part the angels had in her safety. When I think of the protection she received, I cannot help but remember what Luke said, "He shall give His angels charge over you, to keep you" (Psalm 91:11).

A Trial with Sickness

The first week of November 1991, I drew aside for a period to reflect on all I had encountered during the past year. Many of the supernatural things I encountered kept coming back to my thoughts. I focused on the trances and supernatural visitations that had occurred and I began to see the majority had occurred during a time when I was spiritually a bit low. I was still very excited with all that God was doing but I had begun to feel very tired and sick. Despite my prayers and faith, I was beginning to be puzzled about my physical health.

Although I believe in divine healing, I decided to see a doctor and found myself seeing the doctor on a weekly basis. My stomach became bitter and I took antiacids like crazy, yet nothing seemed to help. My doctor pushed, probed, and ran every test possible, but none of the tests could determine any particular reason why I felt so bad. On December 15th, I entered the hospital. As I lay in my hospital bed, I kept thinking of the visitation where I was force fed a spiritual substance: "the living word of God," which tasted like honey. Finally, I drifted off to sleep and while dreaming I heard an audible voice say, "Revelation 10." The voice was so profound I was jolted and awakened from my sleep.

My daughter, who had admitted me to the hospital, was also responsible for packing my overnight bag, but she didn't pack my Bible. Of all things, I ended up in a hospital without my Bible! I reached over and opened my dresser drawer to get a phone book and what did I find? A Bible! Thank God for the Gideon's Army.

I quickly opened it to Revelation chapter ten. As I read verses nine and ten, I saw a new revelation.

"But in the days of the sounding of the seventh angel, when he is about to sound, the mystery of God would be finished, as He declared to His servants the prophets. Then the voice, which I heard from heaven, spoke to me again and said, "Go, take the little book which is open in the hand of the angel who stands on the sea and on the earth." Then, I went to the angel and said to him, "Give me the little book." Then he said to me, "Take and eat it; and it will make your stomach bitter, but it will be as sweet as honey in your mouth." Then I took the little book out of the angel's hand and ate it, and it was as sweet as honey in my mouth. **However, when I had eaten it, my stomach became bitter**, he said to me, "You must prophesy again about many peoples, nations, tongues, and kings" (Revelation 10:7-10).

For the first time, I realized my physical ailment might have contained some form of spiritual seeds. I knew God does not make anyone sick, so I was still puzzled.

After 35 days, the hospital released me due to the lack of insurance. During this time, there was a very popular television commercial about having your own "American Express Credit Card." It had a great closing phrase stating, "Do not leave home without one!"

The day of my release, I received a call from the downstairs billing office. A woman asked, "Mr. Young are you aware you do not have any insurance?"

"Yes, I am."

She then asked, "Are you aware that as of yesterday at 5:00 p.m., your bill was $92,000.00."

"No, I was not aware of that." I responded.

She then politely asked, "How do you intend to pay this bill?" I could not resist saying, "Ma'am, you need to know I left home without my "American Express Card." She immediately began to laugh uncontrollably and had to hang up the phone.

Within a few days, I entered a state charity hospital. My stay there lasted five months. Spiritually, I was so bewildered that I was very silent. I did not know what to think or what to say about my sickness.

When my physical condition worsened, the county hospital took me in. Two weeks later, I had to have emergency surgery; I spent a month in the intensive care unit. One doctor told me I had hemorrhaged to death twice on the operating table.

That news disturbed me because I did not remember having an out of body experience as I had read others had. When that doctor came in to check on me, I asked if he was sure about losing me during surgery, and if so, why I did not remember having an out of body experience. He proceeded to tell me that they had pumped twenty four pints of blood into me the first time and eighteen pints the second time. The reason I did not remember anything for a month was because of a drug they had given me to lessen the trauma of my condition, which was so critical. The doctor informed me that my memory needed a good long rest to help promote and speed up the healing process.

I was not a happy camper. After hearing countless stories of other people dying and going to heaven and seeing Jesus, I ended up having Christian doctors who were concerned about my well-being and kept me from remembering possibly one of the greatest times of my life. After leaving that hospital, I received my bill, which exceeded two hundred thousand dollars, forcing me into bankruptcy.

I wondered what God was doing in my life. To have such supernatural encounters and then to become physically sick and loose all I had worked for all my life puzzled my natural mind.

I moved from the hospital into a relative's home, who was living out of state at the time. The first thing I did after moving in was to do a spiritual house cleaning. The house was full of demonic spirits. There was a history of drugs, alcohol, wild parties, including Ouija boards and Tarot card readings for many years. My relatives only ridiculed and laughed at me when I gave a warning of evil spirits. One relative said, "That stuff is only make believe and for entertainment; there is no such thing as demons."

Growing in Experience

After I spiritually cleaned the house, I entered into a time of seeking God. I kept seeking God and spent countless hours every day in prayer, along with Bible study and a time of waiting on God. I really felt the presence of God, but I also had many questions. I knew waiting was the most difficult part of seeking God but I was determined to get as close to God as possible. I was still physically weak, but I was strong spiritually and knew God had saved my life for a purpose.

During this same time, my good friend, Tom Reedy, who was also a pastor, knew about my visitations and took every opportunity to prod me to move on out into the deeper waters of the prophetic and the supernatural realm. He spiritually knew I needed to exercise the prophetic office and gifts God had given me, and his congregation needed to hear the fresh word of the Lord.

As soon as I regained my strength, I spent as much time with him as possible. He was a wealth of encouragement to me and used me often for prophetic ministry. I enjoyed the practice and especially blessing others with the prophetic word of God. I soon became comfortable with prophesying and doing personal call out.

I began to look forward to prophetically ministering on a weekly basis.

I began asking God for the names of the people who were going to be at the meeting—that really stretched me. I did not always get the name correct, but I tried and was willing to be transparent in front of the congregation. Remember the way you spell faith is with four letters "RISK."

It seemed every ministry session was different. At one church where I was ministering, the Holy Spirit told me to have everyone in the meeting wearing the color red to stand to his or her feet. When I did as God instructed, not only a higher level of revelation came forth, but also a supernatural sign of a rushing wind accompanied the revelation. The Holy Spirit had given everyone standing a corporate blessing or a commissioning to a new level of authority by that same Holy Spirit wind. Later on, I found out everyone who stood up that evening were either long time friends or family members.

During this same period, a pastor in the Rio Grande Valley wanted to meet with me. The pastor wanted to know if I was willing to come to his home for several days to visit with him and his family. That sounded like an exciting road trip, so I gladly accepted the offer.

When we arrived it was lunchtime and he wanted all of us to meet at a local shopping center for a big Mexican meal. With his directions, we located the center and found the restaurant.

The weather was beautiful that day, sunny and warm, not a cloud in the sky. As we were walking from the van to the restaurant, I began to feel a fine mist. I immediately remembered the "Shekinah Glory" that came into the Sanger Theater in Pensacola, Florida the year before. Right in the middle of the street, I stopped and lifted both hands towards heaven. Looking up I smiled I was determined I was not going to miss a single drop of God's glory that was falling upon me.

A few moments later, one of my friends yelled to me "Duane hurry up and get out of the street or you will be covered with the overspray of yellow paint!" I dropped both hands, opened my eyes looked up and towards the building in front of me, and I saw two men with spray paint guns just spraying the building as fast as they could. We all had a good laugh at my very colorful experience. Thank God it was washable paint. Sometimes, I guess we can be too spiritually minded and not enough earthly minded. I am sure God also had a good laugh.

By the end of our first day of visiting with this pastor, I was very tired and retired to my room at midnight. I had just lain down when I began to see flashes of multi colored fire falling through the heavens. As I was pondering this scene, I went into a trance and was immediately standing in the kitchen of an elderly Christian woman I always referred to as mom, who had recently moved to Florida. We lived exactly nine hundred miles apart. In the trance, I turned and looked at mom as she was standing next to her kitchen sink washing a teacup. Mom gently held the cup in her left hand as she reached into its mouth and carefully wiped the reservoir with a soft white cotton cloth. She would rub it and closely examine it for any missed spots. Several stains that had accumulated over many years of use were eventually gone as mom kept rubbing the teacup.

Looking up she said, "Son, I am getting this cup ready to put away and not to ever use it again." I smiled at her and shook my head in agreement as I said, "I love you mom and will see you in glory one day." The next thing I knew, I was lying on my back staring out my bedroom window watching fire fall throughout the heavens. The Lord God does nothing unless He reveals His secret to His servants the prophets (Amos 3:7).

The following week, after returning home, I located one of mom's daughters. When I contacted her, I found out she had not spoken with her mother in over five years because of an anger issue. I conveyed the seriousness of my call and encouraged the daughter to visit her mother. If nothing else, at least call her mom and apologize while she had the time to do so.

I made sure she knew that if we forgive men or women their trespasses our heavenly Father would forgive us. However, if you do not forgive men their trespasses, neither will our Father forgive our trespasses (Matthew 6:14-15).

Within a few moments on the phone with the daughter, I realized that was not what I should have said. The daughter exploded and told me I had no business telling her or anyone else what to do. She began attacking the prophetic gift and the revelation that God had given me concerning her mother passing away, then she hung up on me.

Four months later, another close friend told me "mom" had passed away in her sleep. To my knowledge, the daughter never made that phone call.

Not much else occurred during my first visit to the Rio Grande Valley with that pastor and his family. He was very interested in the prophetic, but was not yet very familiar with it. I shared my trance with them and some of the other prophetic occurrences I had experienced. It would later turn out to be a more important meeting than I realized at the time.

10:40 PM

A short time after the road trip to the Rio Grande Valley, I became excited about an upcoming conference. I heard a very accurate and highly anointed prophet was coming to our church to minister. I remembered some of my thoughts and what I anticipated was going to happen when such a man of God came on the scene. I was so wrong on most of what I had imaged. First, this African minister was a white man who spoke perfect English and not a black man who needed an interpreter. That was a big disappointment to me. He was very familiar with our culture and was "Americanized" on top of it all; that was an even greater disappointment. I was anticipating some sort of culturally different prophetic person from whom I could learn through his teachings and ministry sessions.

A good thing did happen. This man of God ministered prophetically to everyone in our church—except me. I was so engrossed in listening to him prophesy to everyone I didn't realize I was the only one who did not get a prophetic word in our small church. I remember all the women in our church shouted with joy when the prophet called out a woman who was the church secretary. She was a very strong Christian and the prophet told her that God was sending her a Boaz. She broke down crying. Everyone thought she was crying tears of joy, but on the contrary, she did not want a husband. Her husband had deserted her and their two sons because of another woman.

I remember sitting in the back of the sanctuary laughing to myself. I thought it was funny that someone would be so upset about getting married. I have heard others get upset or have seen the look on their faces change drastically when they received prophetic ministry. For some reason, some people just do not like God's plans for their lives.

However, over the years I have learned not to judge what God does prophetically. I have learned not to laugh when I hear of someone getting something that I really do not think is a good thing. I have come to realize that I am basing it on my own assumptions and on my own likes and dislikes.

I really should have known better than to laugh when the prophet said God was sending her a Boaz. Some months later, I was confronted by the same woman one

Wednesday night after church. She told that the Lord had revealed to her that I was in fact the "Boaz" that had been prophesied. She felt released having shared what the Lord had led her to say and said she would not mention it again. I had to admit, she was beautiful, intelligent, gifted prophetically, and a mighty woman of faith; however, I was not looking to be married.

Thursday night at 10:40 p.m., I had just finished reading my Bible and prayer time when all of a sudden, the room felt like electricity, and I became weak and could not move from my chair. An angel appeared standing about five feet in front of me and said, "I have come from the throne of God. The Lord says you are to marry Karah Korvette."

As the angel was talking to me, I was having an open vision. In the vision I saw who Karah Korvette was. She was the new secretary at the church. She was the one I had laughed at when the prophet told her she would be getting a husband, a Boaz. The angel and the vision lasted several minutes but his message is lasting a lifetime.

After the angel left, I remained seated and was dumb founded from the shock. I said, "O God, I am not looking to be married, but if that is what you want, so be it." I knew from my experiences that I needed to obey immediately, or I would start rationalizing. I picked up the phone and called my pastor to obtain her phone number. He said, "This late at night, I do not even want to ask you why. I am sensing in my spirit that God has told you something concerning her; is that so?" To his question, I said, "Yes," thanked him for his time and the phone number, and hung up.

I dialed Karah's number. When she answered the phone, I gave her my name and she acknowledged she knew who I was. I then said, "Karah; I just had an angel from the Lord visit me and was told that God wants us to get married! Will you marry me?"

After a long pause, she said, "Yes."

My response was, "Ok, I will see you in church Sunday," and hung up the phone.

That following evening I called Karah and asked if I could come by her apartment and visit with her and Joshua, her nine year old son. She agreed but gave me a certain time when I could come over. After we visited for about an hour, I felt I needed to go back home. During that visit I realized that her son Joshua was a very likeable and well-mannered boy. It was evident Joshua loved the Lord and was walking on cloud nine when he found out that his mother and I were going to get married. His first question was, "Will you adopt me?" Boy, oh boy, it looked like I was going to get more than I knew—I was becoming somewhat uneasy.

The following week I went over to Karah's apartment again to visit with her and Joshua. As I was leaving I paused at the front door for a moment to tell Joshua goodbye and that I was leaving. As I stood there waiting for his reply, an angel appeared standing next to Karah's right side. Karah did not see the angel, nor did she hear what he said to me. However, she said, "All of a sudden the room felt like electricity." The angel picked up my left hand and placed a fiery wedding band on my ring finger. When this occurred, I responded by saying, "I will receive that" and walked out the door.

Karah looked up and asked me, "You receive what? What are you talking about?" I just kept walking, acting as if I did not hear anything.

The following Friday morning Karah gave me some additional news. She said she thought God wanted us to have matching gold wedding bands with a scripture on them from the book of Ruth saying, "...For wherever you go, I will go...And your God, my God" (Ruth 1:16) written in Hebrew and costing $979.00.

I told her I was broke, and the only money I had came from my parents who sent me 100 dollars a month to cover food and gasoline. I was about to see another of the many demonstrations of "Faith" this woman had.

"Oh, I do not expect YOU to pay for them," she replied. "This is ALL God's idea, so, I expect Him somehow to provide them. Let's go look at them this weekend and pray about it...OK?"

After we looked at the rings, she asked that we pray right then in the van sitting in front of the store. After we prayed, I reminded her I did not see how it could happen since I did not have any kind of resources. She just smiled as she said, "That's ok, God will provide."

Monday morning as I was going out the door, my phone rang. A good friend, who had worked for me the prior year when I need extra help, said he had a dream about me the night before. He asked if I would stop by that morning before I got too busy.

Upon arriving at his apartment, he met me at the door with a hot cup of coffee and asked me in. After I sat down he said, "Now, about that dream last night. I was shown to give you this," as he handed me a check for $1000.00. I could not believe my eyes. I thanked him, left there, and went over to Karah's apartment. She was not as surprised as I was, but she was very happy. She said, "I knew God would provide, and I told you so!" Since that time, we both have experienced many supernatural signs following our three month engagement and marriage.

The Lord had given me a vision that same year. He assured me He would always provide for us. The promise is in Genesis chapter twelve, "I will bless those who bless you, and I will curse him who curses you..." During these past eighteen plus years, we have seen and heard of God blessing those who were obedient to His leading. I desire that fruit may abound to your account (Philippians 4:17). "And the servant answered Saul again, and said, "Behold, I have here at hand the fourth part of a shekel of silver: that will I give to the man of God, to tell us our way" (1 Samuel 9:8).

An example of this provision and blessing was our wedding. All our friends came together, gave us a Jewish wedding, and spared nothing in the marriage ceremony and the reception.

As a single man one of my ideas of having a fun-filled evening was to go to a local shopping mall. I would sit on one of the benches located in the center of the huge walkway, and prophesy to anyone and everyone who would receive the word of the Lord—the vast majority of the people to whom I prophesy are total strangers. Male, female, young or old, it did not make a difference to me if they were willing to receive the word of God from me, I was willing to give it to them.

Sometimes as people walked past me, I would just extend my right hand and bless them. Occasionally someone would see me doing this and come over to inquire what I was doing. To answer that question, I leaned into the Lord God even greater, and He would often allow me the privilege of telling them if their name was in the book of life. To my disappointment, only about one out of ten had their name in the book of life. I was even more shocked when I realized these people did not want to accept God's gift of salvation.

One Saturday evening prior to our marriage, I asked Karah and Joshua to join me at the mall. I do not know if that counted as a date. Before we left the mall, I bought us dinner at a Luby's cafeteria. I will never forget that day. When we got to our table, I looked over at Karah's tray and lo and behold, Karah had the very same items on her tray I had on mine. She had not noticed what I placed on my tray, nor did I see what she had placed on her's. Joshua had been between us and she was supervising what he got. I would love to tell you that Joshua also had chosen the liver and onions with greens and a dinner salad, but he didn't.

I was a deliverance minister prior to walking in the prophetic. I taught mostly by telling stories about past deliverances and experiences with the Lord guiding me in ministry. I had heard Joshua tell one of his friends, "my new dad does not have a job now, but his old job was a plumber and then he did delivery stuff." That evening I spent a few hours with him sharing some stories I do not share with the public. Afterwards, Joshua never told his friends I was a "delivery man" again!

Karah and I have had many supernatural experiences together since our wedding. In fact, on our wedding night, the devil sent us a gift. I was already in bed when Karah walked up to the opposite side of the bed. At that very moment, a prehistoric bird with a wingspan of 20 feet wide and 12 feet long flew into our bedroom. It was making a sharp screeching noise and the flapping of its wings made the air in our bedroom resemble the wind of a ceiling fan running on full speed, (we did not have any ceiling fans in the apartment).

Karah jumped backwards in amazement. Pointing towards the demonic spirit, I commanded it to go in Jesus name. At that very moment, it exploded like a firecracker and disappeared. Karah had a pale look on her face. I just smiled and said, "What a wedding gift."

During our marriage, I learned one of Karah's greatest anointing's was teaching in the realm of "Inner Healing and Deliverance." When she teaches these classes, she enters into the second heaven and cancels all generational curses involving witchcraft that can and will hold the believer back in their walk with Jesus. Thank

God, I did not have to wait that long to get set free and begin enjoying life.

She was not only a former president of Woman's Aglow in Fort Mill, South Carolina; she had also filled three United Methodist pulpits in Missouri and Florida. She has always been a highly sought after teacher for workshops and conferences on how to have victory everyday as a Christian, imparting, healing and stirring up the supernatural power to become an overcomer in all the areas of their lives. Her ministry has set many free and has restored many marriages that had fallen on the sharp rocks of everyday life. It is common for the Holy Spirit to identify gifts in the life of whomever she has laid hands on, which often releases that individual into their calling.

Karah is presently writing a book titled, "God Came Suddenly" about our supernatural marriage that was ordained in heaven and worked out on earth. Between being a wife, mother, and writing books, she takes on speaking and teaching engagements. I will not share any more about how God put us together, as you can read all about it in her book. I do want to share one more story about this woman's level of faith when it comes to hearing God.

One day I came home from a meeting and as I was pulling into our parking space, I noticed her car was gone. When I entered our apartment, she was in the kitchen cooking. I sat down at the dining room table and asked her what I thought was a reasonable question, "Where's your car honey?" I am glad I was sitting down when she answered me. "Well, God has been talking to me about a young man I have known for quite awhile. He was one of my eight grade students, and I have been praying for him and asking God what I could do for him. He may have to drop out of college because his $300, 10 year old car died recently. Well, he came by today with a friend and visited awhile and was really in desperate need of a car, so I felt God say to give him mine."

I figured she was joking with me so I waited until after supper and asked the same question. To my surprise, she gave me the same answer. I was shocked and speechless.

It was not until the next morning that I realized she had given her car away. I pointed out to her she had actually given away "our car." Remember, I became half owner by marriage. You know that part of what belongs to her now has become mine and what belongs to me has now become hers. I asked, "What do you intend to do for a car?"

She said, "Well, we have two vehicles and he had nothing and no family. Besides, you hardly fit in it, being so tall. So, honey, if I heard right, it's no problem, God will provide for us—or maybe we will save money by having one vehicle." She continued with, "Remember what the Apostle Paul said in Galatians chapter six, "Be not deceived; God is not mocked for whatsoever a man sows that shall he also reap." Because we have sown a car, we will reap a car when we need a car.

I thought to myself, here we go again. I had never experienced anyone doing anything like this before and to tell you the truth, I did not want it to happen again. I was still in shock and totally dumbfounded by her actions. I prayed, "God, This has got to stop—is she really in faith or am I in a nightmare?" He did not give me an answer until a month later.

For the next month or so, we were using my old work van everywhere we went, and it was in bad shape. It smelled bad; no matter what we put in it to make is smell better, it only got worse. In addition, it really only had two legitimate seats; it was not a family vehicle.

One day, a couple who knew us called and asked if we would stop by their house later that afternoon. We both hoped it would be for dinner but that was not what they had planned. It was a much greater blessing than either of us envisioned. When we arrived the couple told us to come in and join them in the den. The wife spoke up and said, "We have recognized that the two of you have a special anointing of God upon your ministry. We also realize that it is extremely difficult getting started in the ministry without having a good reliable vehicle to go and minister. Therefore, we both have come to the same conclusion. We want to help you get a better vehicle."

They went on to say, "We have a vehicle that we want to give you." Wow that was great I thought. "The only problem is the vehicle we want to give you is not here; it is in another state. We were in Texas, and the car was located somewhere in one of the northwestern states, about 1800 miles away. Before I could say anything else, the couple said, "We realize you do not have the money to go get it, so we are going to pay your bus fare and give you some spending money for a little vacation on the way back with your family car."

Turning to me, my wife grabbed my arm and whispered, "See, I told you God would provide a car for us when we needed one." I was standing there with my mouth wide open in unbelief. I could not fathom all that was happening. It was all a total surprise to me. Within three weeks we were back home with our new two year old General Motors sedan, which was in like new condition with only 50,000 miles on it.

Sweet Times of Learning

I began my day with prayer and Bible study as usual and was having a tremendous day with the Holy Spirit. It was not long before I found myself musing over "How sweet are God's words to my taste, Sweeter than honey to my mouth" (Psalm 119:103). I pondered this one particular verse...until the Holy Spirit opened it up with a fresh revelation.

As I was writing down the revelation, my newly acquired nine year old son asked to go outside to play. He was out only a few minutes before he rushed back into the house. He kept pointing outside saying, "Dad!—Bees! Dad, go look at all the bees!" When we went out to investigate his request, we found a huge swarm of honeybees and a beehive that was over two feet long and one foot in diameter just above my bedroom window. The beehive had not been there earlier that morning or we would have noticed, because we had to walk right by there to get to our car. We had to get the city's pest division to remove the bees and hive. Later that evening the Lord said, "When you pray in the spirit the same thing occurs, honey comes forth."

"Now all the people of the land came to a forest; and there was honey on the ground, when the people had come into the woods, there was the honey, dripping; but no one put his hand to his mouth, for the people feared the oath. But Jonathan had not heard his father charge the people with the oath; therefore he stretched out the end of the rod that was in his hand and dipped it in a honeycomb, and put his hand to his mouth; and his countenance brightened" (1stSamuel 14:25,27).

In the book of David, it is evident that the word of God is the honey of His word and will illuminate our spiritual eyes allowing us to see the path of life correctly. The word of God is a candle to my feet and a spotlight unto my path (Psalm 119:105).

His word is sweeter than honey; it will always open our spiritual eyes to the greater things in the earth and in the spiritual realm. Eating the scroll was the commissioning of Ezekiel into the office of a Spiritual Watchman, which is another name for a prophet.

"Moreover He said to me, "Son of man, eat what you find; eat this scroll, and go, speak to the house of Israel. So I opened my mouth, and He **CAUSED** me to eat that scroll" (Ezekiel 3:1-3; 3:17; 33:7).

The word used is "CAUSED." The dictionary defines the word "cause" as, "a person or thing that makes something happen or exist or is responsible for something that happens."

At times believers may be force fed the word of God to prepare them for what is about to come upon the earth. There is power in the sweet honey of the word of God, which enables the believer to overcome all things in Christ Jesus. Jeremiah 15 gives the account of Jeremiah eating the word of God. Psalm 119 tells us that David ate the word of God and it was sweeter than honey in his mouth. The book of Revelation gives the account of John's commissioning into the office of a prophet, which involved him eating the word of God.

"So I went to the angel and said to him, "Give me the little book." Then he said to me, "**Take and eat it**; and it will make your stomach bitter, but it will be as sweet as honey in your mouth." Then I took the little book out of the angel's hand and ate it, and it was as sweet as honey in my mouth. However, when I had eaten it, my stomach became bitter, he said to me, "You must prophesy again about many peoples, nations, tongues, and kings" (Revelation 10:9-11).

By the grace of God, I have ministered to a countless number of people many times since those early years as a believer. The largest group I have stood before was just under a thousand, and by His grace and that alone, the fearful man, which is a man pleasing spirit, is no longer a part of my life. The blessing of Jesus is wonderful. Every time I minister, I have been reminded I need to pay close attention to my message, because the words of honey come forth when I least expect them and they are a reminder for me as well.

Healed of a Fatal Disease

Six months after we were married, my wife and I were ministering at Five Fold Deliverance Ministry. Karah gave her testimony about God sovereignty putting us together as husband and wife. Afterwards, I taught on the prophetic and did personal prophetic call out. As I was stepping off the platform, Karah motioned for me to remain there. Walking up to me she whispered in my ear, "Call out cancer and do what God told you!" It is not polite to disagree with your spouse in public especially in church but I did.

She said, "If God said it, then He will back it up. If you do not call it out, then I will." I reluctantly agreed to do so. Stepping back behind the microphone, I asked, if anyone had cancer or any other fatal disease? The entire time I was hoping no one would respond to the invitation. To my dismay someone did. From the very back of the room an old man, I had not seen during the entire ministry session raised his hand. He was in a wheel chair and his wife began to push him forward. As they began to come forth, I stopped them by saying, "Sir, you do not need to come up here. I cannot heal you. I could not heal a flea with a headache. I cannot do anything but declare the decree of the Lord over you." Then I stretched forth my right hand and declared, "The Lord Jesus had suffered and died for your healing and deliverance and I command all forms of cancer in this man's body to leave in Jesus name Amen." After that meeting, we got into our car and headed out to our next meeting in the Rio Grande Valley of South Texas.

While in the valley, Karah and I ministered as usual. She and I taught on the prophetic and did some personal call out. As I was leaving the platform, Karah reminded me to "Call out cancer and do what God told you to do!" Once again, I reluctantly did so. Four days later, we arrived back home late and physically tired. We brought in all our baggage and went over to check our messages. The recorder showed more than 25 phone messages. We realized that 21 of the messages were from the elderly man with cancer who I had declared the decree of the Lord over before leaving town.

This elderly man's disease had begun to eat away at his flesh from the inside. A portion of his groin had deteriorated. His doctor had told him no surgery could help him.

When he got up Monday morning, everything had grown back. The man immediately called his doctor who agreed to see him that afternoon. Upon arriving at the doctor's office, the medical staff was surprised to see the elderly man was not in his wheel chair and was walking without any assistance. When the doctor examined him, he could not believe his eyes. The doctor said he did not know where the cancer had gone and under the circumstances, he could only say the man's disease was in remission. The elderly man said, "Doctor, it's not in remission. My rotting flesh has grown back and there is no pain or lumps. I no longer have a disease, Jesus healed me! That disease was a demonic spirit and it went back to hell to the one who sent it, that is where it went."

There were two blessings revealed to me that day. First, the elderly man's cancer was gone; and the second blessing, I now had a new level of faith and understanding I had never encountered before. Since that day, I have prayed for many who had a fatal disease. I would like to say everyone received healing when I ministered the decree of the Lord. However, I would be lying. I do not know why one person receives their healing and the person sitting next to them does not.

It is not a lack of faith on my part and I do not believe it is a lack of faith on their part. We know that healing is progressive; the elderly man did not obtain his miracle until the second day. Some have reported their healing came in three days, others, seven days passed before their healing manifested and for some it took two weeks and even three weeks. In addition, I do not know why some received their healing sooner than others. I do not know why some never receive their healing at all. I constantly ask God to give me that answer.

One man left the hospital 100% healed three days after receiving prayer. The hospital staff and doctors were amazed. A month later he fell into a deep depression over his medical bills because he did not sufficient insurance coverage. His wife later told us her husband had gotten so discouraged he said, "I wished I had never gotten healed. I should have stayed in the hospital and died. I want to die. Then, at least you would have the money to pay the hospital bill with money left over from my death policy."

A week after he made that confession, the disease returned and ate through a main blood artery in his neck. He died at his home within a few minutes. We can have whatever we say, so be careful what you are saying. You just may get it. Every disease is a demonic spirit. Once it is gone, do not ask it to come back. Stay healed. Everyone has the responsibility to fight a good warfare when it comes to confronting the evil one.

"When the unclean spirit is gone out of a man, he walketh through dry places, seeking rest; and finding none, he saith, I will return unto my house whence I came out. In addition, when he, cometh, he findeth it swept and garnished. Then goeth he, and taketh to him seven other spirits more wicked than himself; and they enter in, and dwell there: and the last state of that man is worse than the first" (Luke 11:24-26).

The relative of a good friend was fifteen miles away in a hospital dying of an incurable disease. Friday night at 11 p.m., we all agreed in prayer declaring the decree of the Lord over him. Saturday morning my friend received a call from his relative who was shouting, "I am healed; I am healed!" He went on to say the night before around 11 p.m. an angel appeared to him called him by name and told him the Lord Jesus Christ had healed him. That afternoon his doctor dismissed him from the hospital.

Two weeks ago, the wife of a good friend of ours died of cancer. I had declared the decree of the Lord over his wife several times yet her body weakened more every day. She was a woman of faith yet she went on to glory. We do not know why God did not heal her. We do know she is in Glory with Jesus.

Babysitting a Cat

A friend asked if we would do a special favor for her and of all things; it was to babysit her cat while she went to Florida. We agreed and drove two hours up into the mountains to her home. In a way, this was more than just to do a favor; it was having a little vacation for us at the same time. We had visited her in the past and had always enjoyed the trip as well as the time we spent at her house. After lunch we kicked back to relax and catch up on some past due reading.

As I opened my book, I kept having the impressions of a snake slithering around in the house. I wasted no time with the idea and shook it off. Later that evening I opened up the trundle bed, which did not lock into place, so I just left my side in the downwards position on the floor. My wife took the fixed side of the bed, which was at normal height. She had just made coffee for the morning and put the cat in the back bedroom when I had a vision. In the spirit, I saw the snake slithering around in the house. This time I said, in Jesus name, I bind you, you foul demonic spirit and I lose you from your assignment. With the same breath I shouted aloud to Karah to let the cat out of the bedroom.

The next morning we loaded our car and made the trip back home. Our friend arrived back at her house with jet lag. Around noon, she entered her bathroom to freshen up when she noticed her black cat lying in the corner of the bathroom. When she bent over to pet it, she had an uneasy feeling and stopped. She turned on the bathroom light and screamed. Coiled up in the corner was a five foot snake. Although it was non-venomous, it was still a frightening ordeal for her.

She called the fire department, the sheriff's department, and everyone else she could think of, but no one would come remove the snake. Finally, a neighbor came over and managed to remove it. When asked what he did with it, the neighbor said, "Oh I just let it go on the back porch and watched it slither away out of harm's way. You need to know those snakes are good; they eat mice and bugs you do not want in your house. Our friend was grateful but unhappy the snake was not disposed of properly with a gun! My motto as well as hers is "a good snake is a dead snake."

That evening she phoned us and told us all about the excitement. After hanging up the phone, I told my wife we would have had more excitement than she if the snake had crawled up on her or me during the night (Psalm 91:11-13).

We as believers must become sensitive to the slightest impressions the Holy Spirit give us. Such impressions can save us a lot of stress and trouble. The Lord speaks in a still small voice (1 Kings 19:12).

The Oil of Separation

In 1994, my wife and I arrived two days early for our graduation at Christian International. We wanted to do some sightseeing as well as have a look around their new grounds and building. Upon arriving at their main offices, we waited in the front foyer until our counselor could meet with us. As we stood waiting, suddenly an angel appeared standing on my right side and poured warm oil all over my head, which ran down my face and onto my shoulders. I said, "Honey look at me." Turning towards me, she saw oil in the natural running down my face and dripping onto my tee shirt. It was obvious that the Lord had sent an angel to anoint me with oil of separation.

Since that day, many times when I minister, the oil appears again on my forehead. I sometimes wipe some off and anoint whoever is receiving ministry.

Recently, the oil began to appear even when I minister to people over the phone. This is a sign and a wonder; I wonder what action may have brought it on? I am still wondering what it all means. Every time I think about the oil running over my head and down onto my face and shoulders, I remember what the Psalms (the book of David) say.

"Behold, how good and how pleasant it is for brethren to dwell together in unity! It is like the precious oil upon the head, running down on the beard, the beard of Aaron, Running down on the edge of his garments. It is like the dew of Hermon, Descending upon the mountains of Zion; for there the Lord commanded the blessing — Life forevermore" (Psalm 133).

This is "The Oil of Unified Separation." The Lord had given everyone a command to come out from among the world. We are in the world but we are not to have the world in us. The moment a person becomes born again, they are a blood washed child of God. They are to live a life separated from sin and separated for service. This is an anointing of separation.

Most people think to be separated from sin means to stop smoking, drinking, cursing, going to bars and ungodly parties etc. It is good to stop all of that but that is not what the oil of separation is. Many people think to be separated means a bunch of 'do not's, which is only a small portion of what it truly means to live a life separated unto God. The Lord told the prophet Jeremiah

"Therefore thus says the Lord: If you return, then I will bring you back; and you shall stand before the Lord your God; if you take out the precious from the vile, you shall be as "My mouth." Let them return to you, But you must not return to them'" (Jeremiah 15:19).

These two things go hand in hand. The oil of unity every believer enters represents the finished work of Jesus at Calvary. This is the anointing oil which bringing forth unification in and to the universal Body of Christ. The Lord expects His leaders to live a separated lifestyle. We all need separation from incorrect theology and the religious traditions of the elders or spiritual leaders of our day.

When we freely choose to live a separated life unto God the Father, Jesus the Christ, and God the Holy Spirit, we have aligned ourselves to inherit the promises and blessing directly from His Kingdom. We must remember when the praise goes up, the miracles and blessings come down. Our separated lifestyle is also worship and praise to God as we come out from among them and become separate, says the Lord. Not touching what is unclean, and He will receive us (2 Corinthians 6:17).

This does not mean you are to separate yourself from the fellowship, meetings and gatherings with like believers. It means that fellowship with God is the most important aspect of our life.

"Father God, I ask You to send your angel with the Oil of Separation and anoint my brother and sister totally unto you, setting them apart for the Spirit of God to flow through them to touch the hurting and the lost. I ask that every one of them will live a separated lifestyle, and not compromising their spirit, soul, or body in any way in Jesus' name. Amen.

A Malachi 3:16-18 Teaching

I once prepared for a ministry assignment by doing a three day fast. I remember as I stood before the large congregation, I felt the presence of the Lord enter the room and I heard the Holy Spirit say, "Read aloud Malachi chapter 3 verses 16-18."

"Then they that feared the Lord Spake often one to another: and the Lord hearkened, and heard it, and a book of remembrance was written before him for them that feared the Lord, and that thought upon his name. They shall be mine, saith the Lord of hosts, in that day when I make up my jewels; and I will spare them, as a man spareth his own son that serveth him. Then shall ye return, and discern between the righteous and the wicked, between him that serveth God and him that serveth him not" (Malachi 3:16-18).

After reading it very slowly to the congregation, I had the people stand up and pair off, telling them to speak aloud the names of unsaved loved ones, friends, relatives or anyone's name that came to their mind. They did this for a few minutes and then sat back down. The Holy Spirit said, "Tell them, every name they called out would receive salvation."

Before leaving that Texas Assembly of God Church, I asked the pastor to follow up on the Malachi ministry session. I asked if he would let us know how many people came to the Lord.

Three months later the pastor notified us that he had had over 100 visitors who repeated the sinner's prayer and more than half of them joined his church since our time with them. Praise God!

Since that day, I have ministered on Malachi 3 in many other churches. Every time I of heard positive results of salvation and new members coming in.

I do not have a corner of the market on the Malachi ministry. To everyone of you out there; it is now time to call the lost into the Kingdom of God. The time is getting shorter every second that goes by.

"Lord God, everyone who steps up and calls out the names of unsaved loved ones, friends, relatives or anyone's name, I thank you in advance You will hear those names and put them into Your book of remembrance and on that day they will become Your special "jewels."

One time while ministering at a small South Texas church the pastor commented that no matter what they did their church did not grow in numbers.

While I was speaking, the Holy Spirit gave me their answer. Walking over to the wall, I pointed to a city map and instructed them to draw a circle representing a five mile radius around their churches' location. Then they needed to list every church in the circle and begin praying for those churches on a weekly basis. The Lord says, "Your church will double in size if you do this."

They did and their church doubled in size that same year. To my dismay, shortly after it grew in size, that pastor moved and his replacement did not feel called to the hurting and homeless. The church dwindled down to nothing and eventually closed its doors.

I have many other stories we have experienced when we ministered out of Malachi. Every experience is mind boggling to us. This is still a weapon in our spiritual arsenal that I use as the Lord leads.

The South Texas Adventure

The year we married, Karah and I moved to South Texas and became co–pastors in a spirit filled church. We also started a school of the prophets.

We both quickly learned that the summers are extremely hot in South Texas. It was 104 degrees by 8:00 in the morning. We learned to do all our outside actives early in the morning or late in the evening. We were doing just that when I encountered another surprise from God.

My precious wife is one of those exercise buffs. She is into walking outside and on the treadmill in bad weather. She believes in eating healthy foods. She is also very organized, so she made us a schedule. Notice she made the schedule not me. Up every morning at 6:30 a.m. and out the door at 7 a.m. on a three mile walk. I am not into walking, especially in hot weather or anything that resembles hot weather. I was not a happy camper on our three-mile walk at 7 a.m. I did know the Mexican food I enjoyed was adding up to some extra pounds, and the walk would help me enjoy the food longer without dieting, as well as give me more energy.

One day we were walking next to an irrigation canal. It was between planting seasons, and you could see five miles in every direction. In fact, I commented that there was nothing out there to look at. No one in their right mind would be out here in the middle of a dirt field walking at 7 a.m. All of the irrigation canals are cemented troughs, connected together for miles and miles. The canals have no end to them and they go on in every direction you look. Because it was between planting seasons, none of these canals had water in them.

This particular day, I was mumbling, grumbling and complaining about having to walk. As I said once again, "No one in their right mind should be out here walking at this hour." My wife paused, looked in every direction and said, "We are!" with her little smile. She motioned for us to continue on, saying, it was only two more miles to the house. For the next ten or twelve steps I was looking down at the ground kicking dirt clods. When I looked up, I saw a man walking toward us approximately ten feet away. My wife was two feet in front of me when I heard her say, "Hi" and heard him return her greeting.

As he approached me, I noticed he was wearing high top lace up boots, khaki walking shorts, an unbuttoned khaki shirt, and a wide brim khaki hat. As we passed each other he said, "Duane, why don't you enjoy the cool breeze and the beautiful sound of birds singing?" As these words were coming out of his mouth, a breeze began to blow and somewhere I could hear birds singing. When we were shoulder to shoulder I replied, "Why don't you mind your own business!" I looked down and went back to my mumbling, grumbling and complaining.

We went on a few steps further when my wife stopped and tapped me on the shoulder and asked, "Hey, how did he know your name?" We both turned around to get a second look in hopes of identifying who he was. To our amazement, he was nowhere in sight. As I had earlier said, there was no place to hide for miles in every direction. We were both standing there with our mouths gapping open when my wife exclaimed, "He was an angel! God sent an angel to tell you to enjoy your walk!

Wow! He was a stranger, and I forgot to entertain or even consider his gracious words that he spoke to me (Hebrews 13:2). I missed a day of my visitation because my focus was only on my personal wants and desires not God's. I have learned to be more flexible and open-minded.

I spent the rest of that day apologizing to God for telling one of His special messengers to mind his own business. That incident was over seventeen years ago. I truly hope I am further along in my Christian walk and to not judge another so quickly or speak so harshly to anyone. My wife reminded me God likes us to enjoy his creation and to get some exercise while doing so.

We began doing a School of the Prophets Class and teenage girls made up the majority of our class. It was great. Several of the young teens could drive nails with their prophetic words and that made both of us proud. God had anointed every one of them and they were all advancing well. However, everything came to a sudden halt for me when I encountered a spiritual attack on my right eye.

We were sitting on our couch, visiting with the pastor and his wife when my right eye filled with blood. The local eye doctor sent me to a specialist fifty miles away. That night I underwent emergency surgery. My retina had torn in five places. Two years later, I went completely blind in that eye. I have had several prophets and apostles tell me the Lord had revealed to them the day will come in this lifetime when I would have that eye restored, and both eyes would have no less than 20/20 vision without glasses.

During this traumatic time of recovery from my eye surgery, I received a prophetic word that the Lord was going to visit me on August 8. That day, I made sure I was available for anything God wanted to say or do. I did not want to miss this day of my visitation because I had begun my radical walk with Jesus when the audible voice came to me in February 1979. My wife and son were also present when the word of the Lord came August 8, and told us to move to Charlotte, North Carolina. The three of us were sitting in our living room that morning and heard the audible command from the throne room (1 Samuel 3).

We obeyed it as quickly as possible. We resigned our appointment in south Texas and moved to North Carolina. Within a few short months, we found ourselves ministering prophetically on a weekly basis at Morning Star Ministries. We submitted ourselves to their teachings and began ministering as prophetic team leaders. I really enjoy prophesying, especially to strangers. Because of that, I volunteered to work the coffee counter and to greet everyone arriving at the meetings each Friday night. During each meeting, I made over six hundred cups of coffee and every time someone stood still long enough, I gave them the word of the Lord.

Spiritual Forefathers

At one of the Morning Star Conferences, Rick Joyner preached a message about honoring your spiritual fathers and mothers.

"Honor your father and your mother, that your days may be long upon the land which the Lord your God is giving you" (Exodus 20:12; Ephesians 6:2).

As he was releasing his message to the Friday night S.O.S. meeting I had an overwhelming urge to visit William Branham's gravesite in Jeffersonville, Indiana. I told my wife about the desire and she reminded me we had a free weekend coming up and could make the drive and visit over the weekend. We immediately arranged to go; we packed our bags and set the alarm for 5 a.m. the following Saturday. As I stepped out my back door, I had a vision of a mother bear and two cubs. I told Karah to drive because I wanted to look for the bears. We were in Jeffersonville by that afternoon, and to my disappointment, we did not see any bears on the trip to Indiana.

It took about an hour to find the cemetery and his gravesite. The gravesite was marked off with a white chain separating William Branham's burial site from everyone's. I walked over to the site and stepped over the one foot high white chain fence and walked up to the monument to read the grave marker. When I was about seven feet from the huge four sided Pyramid grave marker, the power of God hit me. I fell to the ground with the feeling of electricity surging into my body.

My wife ran over to me not knowing why I fell to the ground. When she was within a few feet of the gravesite, she fell to the ground, experiencing the same powerful anointing. A half hour later, we both were able to get up and walk to our car. To this day, we do not know exactly what happened to us that sunny afternoon, but it was God and it was good (Nathan 1:7; James 1:17).

We found a hotel room later that evening and had a good night's rest. We lingered around town for a short time talking about our experience before leaving to go back home. After having a hardy breakfast, we headed back to Ft Mill. I told Karah I wanted to drive home. I had not been behind the wheel thirty minutes when she said, "Oh look Honey, three bears, a momma bear and two cubs over there on the rocks." I stopped the car on the side of the highway and backed up, but I did not see anything. They had moved on. As I drove away without seeing the bears, I heard the Lord say one word, "Patience." I would have seen the bears if I had not become anxious and mixed my faith with patience (Hebrews 6:11-12).

I Kings 19:19

This story will help show how God speaks to His children on a daily basis. If we will pay attention to the circumstances that surround our daily lives, we will soon begin to hear the voice of God.

After moving to North Carolina for a second time, I met a man who asked if I would consider mentoring him in the prophetic. I was reluctant to give an answer either way without first hearing from God. I told him I would get back with him later that week to give him an answer. As I was walking out the door from our meeting 1 Kings 19:19 came to mind concerning Elijah throwing his mantle over Elisha, which was a sign of mentoring.

On the way back home, my wife called and asked if I would pick up hamburgers for lunch. After placing our order the server said, "That will be $19.19" as she handed me my ticket. Glancing down at the ticket, I noticed the ticket number was also 1919. NO—NO God, please; this is not really how I was expecting to spend my summer.

After lunch, I retired to my backyard patio for some solitude and spent the rest of the evening in prayer. I did not want to mentor anyone for any amount of time. Nevertheless if it was the will of God, so let it be. I knew the dollar amount ($19.19) and the ticket number (1919) were not by chance or coincidence. I ended my prayer by asking God if this was really His will for this man, and I to spend some time together studying. I asked God to send me just one more confirmation with the number 1919.

At 8 a.m. the next morning, my phone was ringing. A pastor was calling to tell me he had been flipping houses on the side to help generate an income for his church. In addition, he said, "Brother you would not believe it but I am standing in a home built in 1919. This house is in bad shape, so I am not buying it. Hey, I have to go for now; I will call later this evening, bye."

That was God's answer, but that was not what I wanted to hear. I called the man, and we began meeting twice weekly. He was self–employed, which enabled him to meet almost any time so we chose a local fast food restaurant, and went for it. After several months, I realized he was not benefiting from our meetings. It appeared all he wanted to do was hear my prophetic stories and repeat them to others.

I kept encouraging him because I saw his calling as "A Market Place Minister" who had many opportunities to step out and minister; unfortunately, he was reluctant to do so. I kept in mind the words of wisdom concerning faith and works. Faith only works by love and our actions establish our faith. Just as the body is dead without breath, so also is our faith dead without good works

(James 2:22, 26). My brother in the Lord kept confessing his faith in the prophetic but his actions did not line up with his words. After a while, I lost hope and was discouraged because I did not see any spiritual hunger in him.

I found myself on my face on the floor before the throne requesting a release from the assignment. I had a strong impression to finish out the year and then stop the teaching/mentoring. That is what I did.

Every time we visit Charlotte, I have asked others about this same man only to find out he had sunk further away in his walk with Jesus Christ (Matthew 10:32-33; 15:8).

Divine Humor

During the many years we were at Morning Star Ministries, I had the privilege of meeting many great men and women of God. One of these spiritual giants is the prophet Larry Randolph. Although I never had the occasion to personally meet and visit with him, I quickly learned he had a good sense of humor. Humor is something I look for in the men and women of God. Over the years I have noticed the majority of the leadership is so uptight they have forgotten to take the time to stop and laugh—even if it is at themselves.

I have learned by observation Larry Randolph is a man that not only takes the time to laugh, he goes out of his way to find joy and laughter in any situation that arises. I first met Larry Randolph in 1997, when he found out I was helping at the registration table. He asked if I could get him a name badge with the name of Paul Cain.

Please keep in mind no one who is a speaker needs an identification badge, nor does anyone associated with the Morning Star leadership need a name badge. The reason Larry Randolph wanted a name badge was to interject a little humor when he spoke that evening. I do remember it brought humor to his teaching that evening along with a lot of laughter from the conference attendees.

A year later during a second conference, Larry Randolph again asked if I would get him a name badge with Rick Joyner's name on it. I assured him I would and I set out to obtain one. It was not easy convincing the manager of that department to make me a badge with Rick Joyner's name on it, but I finally succeeded.

With the name badge in hand, I immediately went over to where Larry Randolph had been, but he had left and they did not know the time of his return. I knew I would ultimately catch up with him before he spoke that evening so I just dropped Rick Joyner's name badge into my left shirt pocket. For the next four hours, I felt an electrifying surge penetrate my chest. It was awesome; it was a special anointing from God. I reached down and removed the name badge and the sensation stopped. I placed the name badge back into my shirt pocket and the electrifying surge began all over again. I do not know what all happened that day, but I do know I received some type of an impartation.

"And it shall come to pass in that day, that his burden shall be taken away from off thy shoulder, and his yoke from off thy neck and the yoke shall be destroyed because of the anointing." (Isaiah 10:27).

When I saw Larry Randolph that afternoon, I really did not want to give up the name badge, but I did.

I do not want to imply I know all that God is doing through supernatural manifestations I encounter. I do know they are of God and they are God ordained. I want every one of these spiritual encounters that God will allow me to have. No one can enter into the presence of God and remain the same. Help me heavenly Father not to run out of faith or patience today so I will inherit your precious prophetic promises.

The anointing of God is not a respecter of persons; it will fall on you as fast as the next man or woman. Get under the spout where the anointing is coming out. You may have to travel to a conference (even in another state) to get under that spout. Count the cost (what are you willing to give up to enter into the anointing of God).

Your daily routine lays the foundations of your future. God honors every free will offering and sacrifice you give to Him. The greater the offering or sacrifice the greater your reward will be. When you want something you have never had, you will always have to do something you have never done. You will only possess what you are passionately pursuing.

"Father God I ask that you will give all of my readers some of these same divine supernatural encounters as you have given me. I ask this in the name of Jesus Your Son Jesus the Christ. Amen."

Smiting the Enemy

Whenever I come under a spiritual attack, I strike back. Normally I pull out my cell phone, or my day timer or the stack of business cards that I have accumulated during the past years and I prophetically decree the word of God over that person.

I will prophesy over every name in my day timer and very often I will type the word out and mail it to the individual. This is fun and I have even had my daughter join me at times. I use this as prophetic training for her.

Once I struck back by randomly declaring the decree of the Lord over 88 names from our newsletter mailing list. Within several weeks, we began getting positive feedback from many who received their fresh word.

Many times I will pray and prophetically decree the word of God over the huge collection of business cards I have accumulated.

I will prophesy over every name in my cell phone. When I do this, I normally just call the individual and give them the word of the Lord. If they are not answering, I leave a message on their voice mail (which is best).

At times, I have gone to a local mall and everyone who walks past me will get a prophetic decree from the Lord.

Many times, I do what I refer to as blindfold prophecy. On slips of plain paper, I write the names of everyone our family knows. Next, I fold and tape the slips shut where I cannot see whose name is on the inside of the slip. Next, they are randomly placed into a container and shaken up; as I take the slips out of the container, they are numbered and I then prophesy and (type out all the words) over each number not knowing whose name is on the inside of the slip. After I prophetically decree the word of God over all the slips of paper, I open each slip of paper matching up the name to the number and the prophetic word. I then print out the word and mail it to the individual.

SECTION #4
1996

Translated

Translated—that is right, my wife and I were both translated at the same time. This occurred in Wilmington, North Carolina after Karah ministered on the prophetic at a Baptist Church. We were staying with a friend who lived on the opposite side of town from where Karah was ministering. Because our meeting was on a Thursday evening and Wilmington is a large town, we felt it would be best if we took a test drive to make sure we gave ourselves plenty of time to arrive at the meeting on time.

There were over fifteen traffic lights on College Avenue; the speed limit was 35 mph, and it took us 55 minutes to travel from where we were staying to the church—that was without having to stop for any traffic lights. We understood if we drove 32 miles per hour and were fortunate enough to get the first traffic light on green, we would get all the green lights—providing the traffic ahead of us would be without any hindrances. We decided to eat before the meeting, so we left about two hours early. We made it to our meeting in plenty of time. That night Karah ministered on the prophetic and afterwards released a fresh touch from God to all who were present.

I was surprised when she chose to minister on the prophetic. I personally know one of her major teachings with authority and power was in the realm of healing and deliverance. I have seen meetings where she would lead everyone present through an apostolic prayer that actually broke generational curses from entire families. The spirit of trauma opens the main door for all other evil spirits and addictions to enter. She always rebukes the spirit of trauma before she proceeds to do any form of deliverance. When she ministers in this realm, at times she enters into the second heaven, rips the stolen blessings out of the devil's hands, and returns them to their rightful owners.

When Karah offered to pray for those in need, only two women came forward immediately. Within a few moments there was a line with over fifty people and Karah did not quit until she had ministered to everyone. They received a "Fresh prophetic word" from the throne room the moment she laid hands on them.

When she finished, I went ahead out to the car, carrying her briefcase. As I was waiting in the car, I noticed the digital clock showed 10:20 p.m. The pastor of the church had followed me out to the car and was complaining about how long she had preached. I pointed out we were ready and wanting to leave at 9 p.m., but his parishioners kept coming forward for ministry. He agreed I was correct and it had been a very late night with early appointments for him. We apologized to each other to make sure the devil would not have the slightest crack to enter in and cause a problem.

Karah finally made it to the car and we pulled out of the parking lot at 10:30 p.m. A few blocks later after we rounded the corner onto College Street and spotted a "Donut Shop," we did what all good ministers would do. Not wanting the economy to suffer, we stopped and ate some hot fresh donuts and drank some ice–cold milk. While we were waiting, two women from our meeting called out to us from a nearby booth. They asked us to join them, so we did.

We finished our donuts and milk and left for our friend's house across town. We pulled out of the donut parking lot at 10:55 p.m. We both hoped we were not keeping our host up too late, as it would be well past midnight when we arrived back at our room. We drove the posted speed limit and had to stop for several red lights as we returned to our room. When we arrived where we were staying, I noticed the car clock showed 11 p.m. I tapped on the plastic shell thinking it was stuck. When we walked inside the apartment, we noticed the clock on the mantel read 11 p.m. In fact, all the clocks (four in all) showed the same time.

Karah told her friend there must have been a power failure, as the clocks were all wrong. She went on to state we left the church about 10:30 p.m., went to a donut shop for 20 minutes, and then drove home. Karah insisted the time must be between midnight and 1 a.m. Our friend said, "No, it's only a little after eleven; I was watching the late news and just turned off the TV." We both thought there was no way this could have been true, but it was late and we were all tired, so we all went to bed with the clocks still reading a little after 11 p.m.

To this day, we do not know how the translation occurred, but we were. The following Friday night, after we arrived back at Morning Star Ministries, Rick Joyner announced God had shown him many Christians were going to start being supernaturally translated from one place to another in just a few minutes. We looked at each other and realized that was what we had experienced that very week. It was something very similar to the account in Acts 8:26–40. The Holy Spirit translated Phillip.

A Prophetic Word

One Friday evening as I was entering the fellowship meeting Miss. Intense (not her real name) came up to me and said, "Mr. Young I am desperate to hear from God concerning a situation. Would you please seek Him on my behalf?" I told her to see me after the meeting and possibly God would have something for her.

As I was heading for the door, she stopped me and asked if I had gotten anything. I motioned for her to be still and then I told her the Bible verse the Holy Spirit had given me. She was ecstatic; it was just what she needed to hear.

I opened my Bible and read aloud the verse to her. "Behold, I am with you and will keep you wherever you go, and will bring you back to this land; for I will not leave you until I have done what I have spoken to you" (Genesis 28:15).

She thanked me and turned to talk with another woman who was also leaving the building. I had lingered for a few minutes in light conversation with another friend when I overheard Miss. Intense say to her friend, "Oh, by the way, the Lord has given me Genesis 28:15 for you tonight."

I could not believe what I had just heard her say. As I stood there, the Holy Spirit spoke to me saying, "She just gave her word away to another." I realized the word sown did not go into the prepared soil of her heart; it only penetrated her soul (her mind, will and emotions)—nor was the prophetic word watered and nourished by the living water from the throne of God.

If Miss. Intense would have nourished the prophetic word and watered it, for a week or so, it would have taken root and eventually there would have been fruit (Luke 8:5-7). Then, she could have given some of its fruit to others without suffering loss (Ecclesiastes chapter 3).

The Spirit of Truth

Remember when I told you the way I received salvation and how the "Spirit of Truth" invaded my entire life? From that day forth, I have never been the same person. This is an updated story concerning the wonderful gift of "The Spirit of Truth."

"If you love me you will keep my commandments. And I will pray the Father, and He will give you another Helper, that He may abide with you forever — the Spirit of truth, whom the world cannot receive, because it neither sees Him nor knows Him; but you know Him, for He dwells with you and will be in you" (John 14:15-17).

We accepted an opportunity to minister 27 times in five different non–denominational churches during the following month.

I remember this encounter with the Lord as if it were yesterday. I was driving through Mississippi in the early hours of the morning, pondering what I was going to minister on at the meetings. My mind wondered back to the prior week. We had spent three days fasting and praying at a secluded cabin in the mountains. One evening we had an angelic visitation, which produced feelings of ecstasy and fear at the same time within the both of us. We were full of supernatural anticipation during the next several days. As I drove and meditated on all of this, I heard the Lord speak. He spoke so gently and quietly to my spirit. I almost missed hearing His still small voice (1 Kings 19:12).

"Just ask for the Spirit of Truth." Seven words were all He said. I will confess I was now even more puzzled than ever. "Just ask for the Spirit of Truth." As those words rolled around in my spirit, all of a sudden, it was as if a light came on. I remembered what it meant. I recalled the day the audible voice of God came to me and how the "Spirit of Truth" flooded my life. The spirit of truth is God the Holy Spirit! I reached over, shook my wife until she was completely awake, and told her all I heard and saw in my spirit. She smiled and said, "That's nice honey," and went back to sleep. Even though I was not sure what the Holy Spirit would do when I asked the "Spirit of Truth" to come, my spirit man was flooded with peace just knowing what I was to do at the upcoming meetings (John 14:16-17).

At our first meeting, I ministered on the double anointing of 2 Kings 2:9 and afterwards I did call out prophecy. After the ministry session was over, I asked everyone to stand and be still before the Lord. When everyone was quiet and not moving around, I asked the "Spirit of Truth" to come. Within a few moments, we began to experience God. A woman visitor came forth and said she did not want to remain married to her husband, who was a pastor. I motioned for my wife to come over and assist with the situation. It required more time than we had to give that evening, but within several days before we left town they had their marriage issues worked out and healed.

The second night at the same church, I closed my teaching and ministry the same way. I asked the "Spirit of Truth" to come again. A 15 year old girl came forward and revealed that she was a victim of sexual abuse and incest. After my wife and I prayed for her healing and restoration, Karah took her to the Texas Department of Public Safety. If we hadn't, we would have sent her back into the same situation without any help. The girl agreed to go and tell her story again to the DPS who were extremely unhappy with the situation. As it turned out, the girl's perpetrator was her own dad, who was a local police officer in an adjacent town. The DPS did not like having this problem revealed to the news or to the public. They questioned why the girl told us and not the police.

To that she said, "I knew I would not be treated fairly without outside help and if I just ran away, he would treat my younger sister the same way." Karah stayed with the girl until a caseworker arrived to take her to a safe house around 2 a.m. the next morning.

The next day we were in a different church and town ministering. I again ministered on the prophetic and again did call out prophecy. After the ministry session was over, I asked the "Spirit of Truth" to come. Within a few moments, a young woman stood up with tears streaming down her face. She looked at the man seated next to her and said, "I must confess to you all, we are really not married. We have deceived all of you by implying to everyone that we were." She then turned to the man seated next to her, who by now was trying to scoot down as far as possible without falling out of the chair, and said, "I will not go back to your house with you until we are legally married in the sight of God and man."

That evening after the service, several of us witnessed her live-in companion attempting to kill her by driving his car up onto the sidewalk, attempting to run her down. Fortunately, she saw the car and jumped out of its way. Her pastor and his wife rushed to take care of her and offered her safety with them. For the next several weeks, she lived at her pastor's house with his family. Finally, the young woman and the man became reconciled, received some much-needed counseling, and were married.

I have many other stories that we saw firsthand on that trip. Every experience was a little shocking and mind boggling to us. Each time I invited the "Spirit of Truth" to come, we saw the good, the bad and the ugly. This is still a weapon in my spiritual arsenal that I call upon as the Lord leads me.

Time for Rest

Sometime later, I felt that the Holy Spirit was drawing me to spend more time in the word and prayer. I had already been doing a night watch for several years and was having great success seeking God. In addition, we had planted a church in North Carolina. Every Thursday we drove one hundred eighty four miles round trip to preach and usually arrived back home around 2am. When I mentioned to my wife I was considering another season of fasting and prayer, she said, "Duane, that is all fine and well, but God will not be upset if you took an evening or two off and had some family time on a regular basis." I agreed and made plans to learn pinochle, a card game I had heard about.

We invited another couple over who were in the ministry to help teach us the game. It was our first hand and my partner's wife asked who was going to win? I spoke up and said, "I am." Then she asked, "What are you going to win?" Before I could even give it a thought, the words "A new car" came out of my mouth. I was puzzled why I said those words. Our existing car did have over 200,000 miles and metal fatigue, and we badly needed a new car.

I won the very first pinochle game I had played. The cards were still on the table when our phone rang. It was a couple from Texas. They said, "The Lord had put us on their heart to buy us a new car, so when could you come?" I almost did not believe what I was hearing. Without any hesitation I said, "We will leave tomorrow and be there Tuesday at the latest."

The day we arrived, they told us to go over to the Oldsmobile dealer and pick out any new car we liked. My wife picked out a Oldsmobile Delta 88, and the couple wrote a check for the car. Two days later, we were heading back to North Carolina. On the way back home, my wife had been quiet and thoughtful before reminding me of the car the Lord had told her to give away one month after we were married. Then she said, "This makes two cars we have been given in place of the one I gave away—not bad getting double interest, huh?" (Prisoners of hope today I declare that I will restore double to you Zechariah 9:12). "Now", she declared, "I have enough faith for a house!" All I could do was smile, shake my head in agreement and keep my mouth shut.

Judgment

We were at a prophetic team leaders meeting when Karah volunteered me to minister at a prophetic conference Morning Star was having in Jacksonville, Florida the following month. She knew she could not go due to her schedule, and claimed God told her I needed to go. Her act of generosity created three obstacles for me.

The first obstacle was I did not have transportation to and from Florida. The second obstacle was I did not have a place to stay in Florida, nor did we have the finances, which would allow me to stay at a hotel and rent a car.

During the past five years, we had opened our home to M.S. conference attendees numerous times. We did this to help the less fortunate attend a conference without the additional expense for a hotel room, which was often the major cost. We were always meeting wonderful people when we worked as Team Leaders in the Morning Star Prophetic booths at each conference, and this was a good opportunity to get to know everyone better.

Karah suggested I call the host church with over 2000 attendees and inquire if they had anyone who would put me up during the three day conference since we had "sown into this ministry by providing rooms for others." The church offered to put my name and phone number on the overhead screen before and after each service for the next few weeks. Three weeks went by, and no one offered a room. If they had said a prophetic minister needed a room to stay in while ministering at the upcoming conference, my phone probably would have rung off the hook. My wife insisted she knew I was to go and reminded me that we had sown plenty of seed for this very thing, so we should pray and see it through. I had decided I would withdraw my name if no one offered a room by midweek because I needed to give Morning Star enough advance notice to replace me as a team leader at the conference.

Several days before the conference, a family called my home to tell us I could stay at their house. Everything began to look promising for the trip. I found another team leader who was going who said I could ride with him. The day we left for Florida he was four hours late and "I am a very punctual person." If you say we are leaving at 10 a.m. that is when I expect to leave. It was an eight hour trip to Jacksonville and now we were leaving four hours late without any real explanation. Once we left the city, the vehicle began having crazy electrical problems, and on top of it all, it began to rain. When he turned on the windshield wipers, the headlights would go out. When he turned off the headlights, the windshield wipers began to work again.

We did not arrive at our destination until 11:30 p.m. that night. If the car had not broken down, we would have arrived at 8 p.m. even after leaving North Carolina four hours later than planned. I was not a happy camper. To make matters worse, when I opened my suitcase, none of the contents were mine. As it turned out we had identical suitcases, and he had given me his suitcase by mistake. After imposing on those who had graciously offered me the room, and correcting the suitcase problem, it was well past 2 a.m. before I got in bed.

The next day was an exciting one. There is always a special anointing over a prophetic conference, which surpasses all other anointing's. Those who are attending came with great anticipation of hearing a fresh word from God. Their excitement, combined with all of the prophetic ministers who came to minister at the conference, always creates an extremely high level release of the prophetic anointing.

There were possibly over fifty prophetic team leaders from Morning Star who had come to the conference. I knew all the team leaders and made it my duty to tell them about my entire trip. I went into every little detail about leaving four hours late, losing oil pressure, electrical problems, air conditioner breaking down, and the luggage confusion.

I did my prophetic ministry as scheduled and was bummed out and exhausted at the end of the first day. I noticed my alarm clock read 11:30 p.m., the same hour I had arrived the night before. I removed my shoes and began to unbutton my shirt when I heard a voice behind me say, "You are wanted; come with me." Before I could turn around to see who was speaking to me, I found myself standing in a courtroom in heaven. Looking up at the huge judicial bench, I saw Jesus. He stated, "You are charged with maligning a brother, how do you plead?"

When the Lord asked me, "How did I plead', my mind was racing to find a good excuse or a good reason to make me look good and not guilty. The moment I opened my mouth to give what I thought was a great reason for maligning a brother, my tongue began uttering words on its own saying, "I am guilty as charged Lord, please forgive me." I quickly grabbed my tongue to make it stop. The moment I released it, the same words came out of my mouth a second time. "I am guilty as charged Lord, please forgive me." All I could do was hold my head, and wonder what was next. I could not believe my tongue was confessing to God on its own (Romans 14:11).

The next thing I heard was the Lord saying, "You are sentenced to six months of community service." Looking up at Him, I opened my mouth to question what I heard, when all of a sudden, I found myself standing back in the bedroom, looking at the clock. It was still 11:30 p.m. I turned and sat down on the bed in total amazement with a little bit of fear. My mind was rushing in every direction at once. That night I did not sleep very much. I spent much of the night on my knees in prayer and repenting for maligning a brother in Christ, and reading my Bible.

I now have a greater understanding of our tongue confessing. The next day was the second day of the conference. I made it a point to find everyone I had told about the problems with my trip to Florida and this brother, and repented to them. I finally found the man I had ridden down with, and I apologized to him for being such a jerk. Thank God for the blood of Jesus that enables us to receive forgiveness for sin (James 5:16).

When I arrived back in Charlotte, I told my wife about the ordeal. We both wondered what the Lord meant when He said I was to do six months of community service—especially my wife since she knew that often the spouse suffers with their partner when God disciplines.

We know now. For the next six months, we ministered more than we had for several years and we did not get any financial blessings for any of the ministry. We paid for everything out of our own pocket and did not receive a single dime. That was the six months of community service. It was the hardest six months we experienced the entire time we lived in North Carolina.

I am now extremely cautious of condemning or maligning anyone no matter what kind of situation I may encounter. There is only one Lawgiver and Judge, the one who is able to save and to destroy; but who are you who judge your neighbor (James 4:12).

End Time Ministers

A year later, I had the privilege of returning to Jacksonville, Florida—this time it involved personal business. Our new family of friends insisted I stay with them while in town, which I graciously agreed to. I even stayed in the same room as I did on my first trip to Jacksonville. The first trip was for ministry, and this trip was business, or at least that is what I envisioned.

On the second night, as I removed my shoes I noticed the digital clock showed that it was 11:30 p.m. I reached up and began unbuttoning my shirt when I heard a voice behind me say, "You are wanted; come with me." Before I could turn around to see who was speaking, I found myself standing in heaven in a huge room that resembled a library.

There were angels and people everywhere. In the middle of the room were huge island desk. All the desks had a giant book lying on them. The book on my desk was

24 inches tall, 18 inches wide and 4 inches thick. I turned the book over and opened the back cover. I began turning the pages as if I knew what I was looking for. Every page had various numbers of names listed from top to bottom. Some of the names were in bold gothic print while others were in light delicate lettering. Some names were long, taking up the entire width of the page; other times the opposite was the case with name crammed into a small space; I saw various colors of ink, but the majority of the names were in black or blue ink. As I looked over the names, I asked the angel what these names represent.

He said, "These are the names of end time ministers. The length of the name represents the length of time they will minister; the color signifies various aspects of their calling and gifting."

I kept turning the pages and all of a sudden, I saw my wife's name, Karah K. Young, and I just about jumped out of my skin. I was speechless. I frantically kept turning the pages looking for my own name when the angel said; "we must leave now you have seen all you need to see." I protested and kept turning pages when a second angel walked up to my left side and the two of them said, "Let's go," and the next thing I knew I was standing in my bedroom in Jacksonville, Florida."

I could not help but notice the clock still showed 11:30 p.m. In eternity, there is no such thing as time.

I was excited and disappointed all at the same time—Excited for my wife and disappointed for myself because I did not see my name. After falling asleep, I dreamed there were 26 desks, one for each letter of the alphabet, which contained the different names of the end time ministers. These individuals will be ministering from every continent and nation in the earth prior to the Lords return. Many were names of moms and dads who had trained up their children in the way they should go. Others were friends and family members who took the time to share the gospel with someone in need. The names were not just those of super stars. The names were names of homemakers, mechanics, teachers, bakers and plumbers, and laborers—degreed and non-degreed alike. God is not a respecter of persons (Romans 2:11). The person who does His will, will not be left out or behind in the blessings of God.

The hour was late so I waited until morning to call my wife to tell her the good news. She was excited but said, "Darling the only thing that would make this information better is if I had read both our names."

New Age

Our home is at the base of a mountain and the homes at the top of the mountain are three times the size and five times the price of ours. As usual our move was hectic and everywhere I looked there were boxes and piles of stuff—one pile to keep and one pile for goodwill. It is amazing how every time we moved, we always ended up getting rid of many items. I always wondered why we did not get rid of the items before moving them to our new location.

Because it was a Friday night, we had decided not to look at our mess and relax for the evening. Our daughter was in her bedroom playing her keyboard, watching a movie and listening to a worship song all at once. Now that is multi tasking if you ask me! If I do more than one thing at a time, it takes me five times longer to finish it.

Earlier that day we learned one of the nicer homes on top of the mountain had questionable (New Age) meetings on a weekly basis. This house was on a high spot overlooking thousands of homes below.

As my wife and I kicked back and enjoyed one of those dessert coffees with the chocolate and whip cream, our daughter came in and said, "Someone is outside throwing rocks at my window." We turned the volume down on the television and within a few moments, we could hear dings and pings on the living room windows as well.

I told them not to worry and to agree with me in prayer. I commanded all foul demonic words to fall to the ground and not light upon our home or us in Jesus name Amen (Proverbs 26:2). We also asked the Lord to forgive and save everyone who was attending that New Age meeting (Romans 10:13).

I explained to my daughter that when people release word curses against us they would sound like pebbles or stones hitting our windows. We all asked the Lord to put a shield up around our home and cancel out all verbal attacks in the future. To my knowledge, we have not had a reoccurrence for over two years.

Just before we turned in that night, we noticed a large amount of automobiles descending the mountain as a sign that the Friday night New Age meeting adjourned until another day (Exodus 20:3-5, 7, 16).

Today many of the Lords servants are (spiritually) committing sexual immorality and eating things sacrificed to idols (Revelation 2:20). We do not think of idols in our day especially in America. Nevertheless, be aware false worship and idols are nearly everywhere you turn.

All false religions have one or more false gods behind them that receive the worshipper's adoration and praise along with anything else the individual freely gives.

When we spiritually give our love, our worship, our time, treasure and talents to anyone other than the Lord Jesus Christ, we are spiritually committing sexual immorality. Moreover, we have become intimate with a false god or an idol. A false god or a false religion are the same thing.

When we eat things sacrificed to such idols, we are receiving and digesting words, teachings, deeds or thoughts that have been taught to us concerning the false religion or idol. These so called well organized structured false teachings alter your belief system and promotes the worship of these false gods. During the entire time, these individuals do not realize they have gotten involved in a false religion known as idol worship or an occult.

"Father God, I ask that you to deliver anyone who is reading this book from all forms of false religions and idol worship in Jesus name Amen."

Eternity

Shortly after I received salvation, I heard the Lord say, "I will always tell you where your loved ones are spending eternity." When I received that promise, I did not really realize just how much of a spiritual impact this would have on my entire life and on our ministry.

"Surely the Lord God does nothing, unless He reveals His secret to His servants the prophets" (Amos 3:7).

Along with that prophetic promise and the revelation of where a loved one would spend eternity came a profound understanding of how to live our lives for Jesus Christ. It also gave a greater clarity of how "Not To Live Your Life."

I have had the privilege of seeing my mother in heaven on the day she arrived. She was drinking living water from a diamond wine carafe. Her wedding garment flashed so brightly I had to squint to continue looking at her.

Another time, while I was pondering a scripture, I suddenly found myself in heaven. I was standing under a huge grape arbor viewing a beautiful snow covered mountain ridge in the background. The grapes were as large as softballs; the cluster was three feet long and two feet wide at the top. Their fragrance was indescribable. I was lost in total amazement when I heard a familiar voice behind me saying, "Duane, what are you doing here? It's not your time yet." Turning around I saw a relative I loved with the love of Christ. I had prayed to know if he was in heaven many times. None of these relatives spoke with me nor was I able to talk with them. The angel standing beside me said, "We must return." In the next moment, I was in my living room. I had a wonderful time praising God for showing me where this loved one was in answer to my many prayers concerning him.

To my sadness, I have also accompanied an angel as he delivered another relative into the deepest jail of hell on a different occasion—the seventh level where those who knew the way of God denied Him and returned to a lifestyle of evil, blatant sin.

Another family member told me never to mention the name of Jesus, God, or Holy Spirit to him ever again, or else he would make sure I suffered financial loss. Exactly 24 hours later he died.

Once, I had a call from a family member who asked if God had shown me where a certain relative was spending eternity. "No, I said, but I will ask." Looking up to heaven I said, "God where is this individual in eternity?" The words were still coming out of my mouth when both fire alarms in our apartment went off revealing where they were spending eternity. Later in another vision, I saw this same person in a burning tar pit in eternal pain and punishment.

Another time, I stood at the edge of outer darkness. I found myself standing in total light when I saw a relative coming up out of the darkness. Outer darkness is like a thick, black, tangible smoke filled fog. Just standing next to it, I could mentally feel the loss of breath. It was a very fearful encounter for me. The blackness was like a thick black smoke similar to a campfire smell. The individual was gasping for breath and frantically grabbing for something to hold on to but there was nothing to grab. I saw a look of excruciating fear and torment on his face. Although I saw his mouth frantically moving, I was not allowed to hear his screams. I could see that the individual was naked (Job 26:6) from the waist up, and I knew in my spirit he was completely naked. Then, I remembered the story of the person who was not wearing a wedding garment. Those without a wedding garment will be bound hand and foot, taken away, and cast into outer darkness; there will be weeping and gnashing of teeth (Matthew 22:11-14).

All of these individuals had at one time or another said the sinner's prayer and received water baptism. They had the gospel preached to them many times. I personally witnessed to each of them making sure the plan of salvation was so simple a child could understand, believe and receive eternal salvation. In every direction, downwards and outwards there was total darkness; it was the blackest darkness I had ever seen. I knew this blackness did not have an end to its width, length, depth, or height. When the encounter ended, I noticed the time was **8:07** p.m. I immediate recalled Luke **8:07**: "Some seeds fell among thorns and the thorns sprang up with it (which are the cares of this world, and the deceitfulness of riches, and the lusts of other things entering in, and it became unfruitful) and choked the word of God."

With the earthly understanding of how these relatives lived, coupled with knowing their character and values, it was easy to see why they ended up where they did. I had given a personal warning to all these relatives many times before their departure into eternity.

"When I say to the wicked, 'You shall surely die,' and you give him no warning, nor speak to warn the wicked from his wicked way, to save his life, that same wicked man shall die in his iniquity; but his blood I will require at your hand. Yet, if you warn the wicked, and he does not turn from his wickedness, nor from his wicked way, he shall die in his iniquity; but you have delivered your soul" (Ezekiel 3:18-19).

I had given the good news gospel of Jesus Christ to each relative prior to him or her passing away. I did not want their blood on my hands. Like most of us, our relatives seem to think they know more about God than those whom God sends to warn them.

There have been other times I told individuals they were not going to live another day. I made sure I saw each of them and shared the gospel of Jesus Christ. Two individuals claimed they were Christians and did not need anyone telling them such stuff. Both were living in open sin and to my knowledge did not repent.

The third individual was in a cult. This person became violently angry with me, and began railing at me all kinds of threats, and accusations. He said a good God would not cast anyone into hell. He died exactly at the same hour the following day. I wept all day when I heard about his death. Every man and woman has an appointed time to die once, but after this the judgment (Hebrews 9:27).

I believe a person can die prematurely. There are seasons for everything and everyone. There is a time for every purpose under heaven: A time to be born, and there is an appointed time to die (Ecclesiastes 3:1-2). If a person dies outside of Gods appointed time schedule, it will be an accident, murder, or suicide.

Since I started writing this book I began asking God where a particular relative was spending eternity. This morning the Lord answered that question. While awake, I saw this individual in a vision. He was in what looked like a huge black hole. Then I realized he was alone and in a smoldering tar pit. For a fleeting second I smelled the stench of the hot tar. I watched as the fire burned away at his flesh. Within minutes his flesh reappeared, and the burning process began all over again. He was in extreme agony. I saw and heard pain in every breath he took. It was a horrible sight. What was so sad was when I began sharing the gospel with my relative, he vehemently resisted and insisted he was perfectly content with his faith walk (Genesis 14:10)!

While living in Jacksonville, Florida, the Lord chose to use me to issue one such warning to a lukewarm believer like my relative. It was noon and I had ridden with a friend to a job site he needed to check on. As I sat in his van waiting for his return, the Lord began to speak to me about a plumber who was digging a ditch a few feet from our van. Getting out I went over and introduced myself to him. He stopped digging to hear what I had to say. I said, "Sir, you need to repent for the sin of drunkenness. The Lord showed me you get drunk every night and you repent on Sunday while watching a religious program on television. You will not be alive this Sunday; you need to repent now." After I finished speaking, he said, "I know God, and I am all right with Him, and He is all right with me. We have an understanding; every night I get drunk and I repent every Sunday, so that's that." I tried to tell him again to repent but he refused to listen. A few minutes later, I heard the sound of the vans horn signaling it was time to leave.

That same day at 3 p.m., a friend who was with me received a phone call. From the partial conversation I overheard, I could tell it was not a very pleasant phone call. Hanging up he said, "I hate to say this, but the man you were talking with who was digging the ditch dropped dead an hour ago from a coronary heart attack."

"Again, When a righteous man doth turn from his righteousness, and commit iniquity, and I lay a stumbling block before him, he shall die: because thou hast not given him warning, he shall die in his sin, and his righteousness which he hath done shall not be remembered; but his blood will I require at thine hand. Nevertheless if thou warn the righteous man, that the righteous sin not, and he doth not sin, he shall surely live, because he is warned; also thou hast delivered thy soul" (Ezekiel 3:20-21).

A Cult

Early one morning I had a vision concerning a man in California. Before the day was over the Lord told me to go issue this man a warning. Jesus was going to blot the man's name out of "The Book of Life" if he proceeded with his plans. I told my wife to pack our bags and we headed out. We traveled fifteen hundred miles one way to give the warning.

After we arrived in his town, it took another two weeks before I located him to give the warning. When we met I asked for his testimony. He told me as a young boy he had confessed Christ in a Baptist church and remained there until becoming an adult. After he married, his wife wanted him to join her church to keep harmony in their marriage.

He was in the process of joining a well known religious cult that believed in earning salvation and had major issues involving blood transfusions. This man was going to renounce salvation by the blood of Christ that following Sunday as an act of acceptance into that religious cult (Revelation 3:5).

He admitted his involvement and repented of his sin. Before I left our brief meeting, he rededicated his life to Christ and received the baptism of the Holy Spirit (1 John 1:9).

I went back to my room and told my wife my assignment was over. The next morning we packed the car and headed home.

Barrenness

On more than one occasion, the Holy Spirit has instructed me to cancel the spirit of barrenness in the lives of married couples. Once we asked every woman in the congregation who was barren to stand to their feet. Sixteen married couples (men and women) stood and we cancelled the spirit of barrenness. A year later the pastor sent word twelve couples were now expecting.

In 2009, while eating at a restaurant, the Lord revealed to me that our server was barren. When I asked her about being barren, she admitted that she and her husband had been trying for seven years to conceive a child but were unsuccessful. I took a sip of water, cleared my throat, extended my right hand, and commanded all barrenness to leave her body in Jesus name and that they would be fruitful and multiply.

Three months later we were in that same restaurant. When that server saw us she ran up to our table shouting I am pregnant! I am pregnant! She had a beautiful, joyful, healthy baby girl.

If you are one of those couples, who have been unsuccessful in conceiving and having your own child lift up both hands and receive the blessings of God. "Father God I come to you by Your Son's cross and blood. I stand in the gap for the one who is reading this prayer. I cancel the curse of barrenness in them and in their family linage by the mighty name of the Lord Jesus Christ. Amen. Be fruitful and multiply. Go forth and multiply—faith without works is dead."

A Funeral

I attended the funeral of an unsaved person because I had known the parents and felt my appearance would be a comfort for the survivors (Luke 9:60).

The funeral was in East Texas—the same state I call home. When two of my girls found out I was attending the funeral, they wanted to spend time with me, so they took off work and made the long trip so we could visit.

On the day of the funeral, I walked up and stood beside the casket to view the body. I became aware that a demon was speaking through the corpse. I shook off the occurrence as a lack of sleep or jet lag. When I realized what I was seeing and hearing was spiritually real, I asked God what He wanted me to do if anything at all. Did He want me to cast out the demon or command the dead person to rise up in Jesus name? After a few minutes without getting a specific reply, I decided to leave the demon in the body allowing them to share eternity together.

A few minutes later, I realized that one daughter had walked up and was standing next to me. As a grateful gesture of her attending a funeral she did not need to attend, I reached over and placed my right hand on her shoulder as a gentle gesture.

Within moments she jerked backwards and out from under my hand. A minute later, she again stepped up and was standing next to me. Again, I put my hand on her shoulder. For the second time, she jerked backwards, freed herself from my hand and gave me a strange look as she went and sat down.

My other daughter came up on the other side of me, and when I placed my hand on her shoulder she bolted away and immediately returned to her seat and sat down.

Later that evening one daughter told me she became frightened while viewing the body. "Daddy, everything was ok until you put your hand on my shoulder. That is when I began to hear muffled sounds similar to a human voice, but I could not make out the words. Then, out of the corner of my eye, it appeared as if the dead person's lips were moving. Dad, I know dead people cannot talk or move their lips; I also know that I do not want to see or hear any dead person moan or move, so I went and sat down."

The other daughter said, "Dad, I heard a muffed sound and did not want to hear or see any dead person speak or move." After returning home that evening I went before the Lord for answers to the questions I had about what we heard and saw at the funeral.

Dear reader, PLEASE, PLEASE, PLEASE keep in mind the voice and the lips, which were moving, were in the spirit realm only. The dead person was not moaning or moving in the natural realm. It was a demonic spirit speaking through the corpse and making the lips quiver.

Later that same evening as I waited before the Lord, a verse from II Kings kept coming to my mind: "Then Elisha prayed and said, 'O Lord, I pray, open his eyes that he may see.' And the Lord opened the servant's eyes and he saw; and behold, the mountain was full of horses and chariots of fire all around Elisha" (2 Kings 6:17). This speaks of the spiritual eyes. Because of God's gift at times, I am able to see in the spiritual realm. My daughters entered into that same anointing when I placed my hand on them. That same ability flowed out of me and into them.

When I said a particular Bible verse kept coming to mind, this was how God usually speaks to me—by His written word. His word, will, and way for our lives never changes. God may not always give you a Bible verse to answer your question but I assure you whatever answers He gives you will "Never, Ever Contradict" His written word, will, or way in the canon of scripture.

Both my daughters and I had come under the same type of anointing that Elisha and his servant had encountered. I had not prayed that my daughters or anyone else attending the funeral would experience what I was spiritually seeing and hearing. Several months later the Holy Spirit revealed to me why my daughters saw the moving and heard the moaning. Their call is also to the prophetic office (Ephesians 4:11).

"Heavenly Father I am asking that all those reading this book will come under the Elisha anointing (2 Kings 6:17). Open their spiritual eyes to see into the invisible realm in Jesus name, Amen."

Levels of Demon Possessions

Mark 5 tells the story where Jesus cast out an unclean suicidal spirit from a man who lived naked and dwelt among the tombs. The demons begged Jesus earnestly so He would not send them out of the country. Jesus allowed the demons to enter a herd of swine located on a mountainside. Jesus gave permission, and the unclean spirits went out of the man and entered into about two thousand swine, and the herd ran violently down and into the sea and drowned. The town's people came out to see what happened and found the demon possessed man sitting, clothed, and in his right mind at the feet of Jesus.

The **first** level of demon possession occurs when a demon possesses a human, and they have a greater ability to kill, steal and destroy. This particular demon was a tormenting and suicidal demon. It tormented the man day and night causing the man to cut himself. Scripture indicates the man was naked. Could this be another level of demon possession that prompts men and women to run naked such as in topless clubs, lie in the sun nude, work in strip clubs, or go to nudist colonies? Could this also indicate people who parade around naked have a mental problem? The words "in his right mind" could indicate anyone who is suffering from a mental situation may have demon oppression or possession. Sitting at the feet of Jesus speaks of total submission and servant hood. It is interesting that Jesus told the man to go back to his family and tell them what great things God had done for him. We are to tell our families and friends first—that is our primary mission field.

The **second** level of demon possession involves animals. In this same story, the demons left the man and entered the swine, which in turn committed suicide. How many times have you read in the newspaper or heard on the news of an animal, especially a domestic animal such as a dog, attacking and mutilating a child or even killing a child. All such animals are demon possessed. I love pets but not demon possessed pets and animals. Demon possessed animals must be destroyed before they kill or tear up a human.

The **third** level of demon possession is possibly the most predominate; it is in 1st Samuel 5. The Philistines had taken the Ark of God and placed it into the house of their false god, Dagon. When the false priest of Dagon entered the temple early in the morning, Dagon had fallen on its face to the earth before the Ark of the Lord God Jehovah. The priests took Dagon and set it in its place again. In addition, when the priest arose early the next morning, Dagon had fallen on its face to the ground before the Ark of the Lord again. The head of Dagon and the palms of both hands were broken off on the threshold—only Dagon's torso was left. A demon's last choice is to possess a tangible object such as a statue, an image, a shrine, a picture, etc...

Today many individuals give homage to such demons when they pick up the receiver of their telephone. Some of these individuals are a God fearing, born again person until they put the phone up to his or her mouth.

Years ago the Lord revealed to me the sin of maligning, slander, gossip, and lies had increased over 1000% with the invention of the telephone. This is not a sin just women commit; men are just as bad.

I am not telling you to get rid of your telephone. What I am telling you is to be aware that if a demon has the opportunity to enter it and entice you to malign, slander, gossip or tell lies about anyone it will. I have known some individuals who from time to time will anoint their phone and command all lying spirits to leave their phone and home. In the multitude of words, sin is not lacking, but he who restrains his lips is wise (Proverbs 10:19).

Surprised by an Angel

While living in Jacksonville, Florida, I held on to the habit of using my vehicle as my prayer closet, so I often found myself parking and praying in my vehicle. Daily, when I had a break, I would drive over to a nearby church and park. The shadiest place on the property was on a water retention lane. That was where I chose to park my car and pray or read scripture. Sometimes I would get out and walk around while I prayed. On one particular day it was Pentecost eve about 6:30 p.m. A cool gentle breeze was so refreshing I opened my car door and rolled down all four windows to allow the cool fresh air to circulate and refresh me. Before I began to pray, I decided to adjust the seat into a more comfortable reclining position I recently discovered. I was meditating on what I just read when hunger pains announced it was time to eat.

I poured myself a cup of hot coffee, took my cold sandwich out of the bag and placed it on the sunny dashboard with hopes that it would warm up the bread. The sandwich was still a bit cold, so I waited patiently before the Lord. During this time, I had the impression someone was watching me. I looked in the rearview mirror and then in both directions from the driver's side of my car and saw no one. It was not until I turned to glance out my back passenger window that I saw him! I was so frightened; I yelled and leaped from my car all in one split second. An angel was watching me. My jumping and yelling apparently frightened him as much as his appearance had frightened me. I looked all around but he was no longer there.

After I settled down and my blood pressure returned to a normal level, I felt as if I had missed a great blessing. This thought birthed discouragement, which I had to cast down by confession of the word of God. I chose to believe I would have another opportunity to see and to visit with this same angel.

This angel was what the book of Daniel refers to as "A Watcher Angel," or better known as "A Guardian Angel." This was the first time I saw an angel in the actual flesh and arrayed in his heavenly glory. I normally don't see angels outside of trances, open visions, dreams or when I go to heaven. By now, I was so rattled there was no way I was going to remain parked were I was. I poured out my coffee, repacked my sandwich, closed my car door and drove home. As I drove home, I became aware that I was constantly looking into the back seat. It was as if I was fearfully expecting to look and see the same angel just sitting there. When the angel of the Lord appeared to Zacharias he was troubled, and fear fell upon him (Luke 1:11-12).

My wife was surprised to see me return home so early because normally I would linger at the church until sometime around dark–thirty. As I began telling her about the angel looking in my back passenger window she became excited and joyful. I kept saying to her, "You do not understand, I was frightened by the experience." She just smiled and said, "I believe you will see him again and be spiritually prepared the next time the angel appears." That night I reread Luke 1 and shortly thereafter felt much better about my reaction.

Later, I told my wife things I remembered about this angel. The very first thing was his smile. He had the most beautiful smile I had ever seen. The words had just finished rolling off my lips when I saw the book "Visions of Heaven" by H.A. Baker. I got up from the kitchen table and went into the room where the bookshelf was. After shuffling through the books, I located that particular book. When I picked it up, it automatically opened to page 70. My eyes fell to the middle portion of that page and I began to read, "There is no way on earth to describe an angel's smile." I took the book and pointed out the quotation to my wife. She read it and smiling she said, "You are right."

The second thing I remembered was his teeth. They were the brightest and whitest teeth I have ever seen.

It is 54 inches to the top of my car's roof. This angel had to bend over almost at a 60 degree angle to look into my car window. That meant he was probably over seven feet tall. His pants were a dazzling white and his shirt was a long sleeved pull over the same color of a shiny copper penny. The material resembled the crinkle material I have seen a woman's dress made of.

His appearance was so startling, I did not sleep very well for three days. My wife said, "Honey, God loves you so much, he sent a smiling angel to look in on you!"

Well that was ok for her to say, she was not the one he frightened. I did pray that I would have this or a similar experience again and soon. I believe the Lord has shown me I would have that same opportunity one day, "Thank you Jesus." After that visitation, it was a while before I returned to the same location for Bible study and prayer.

One problem with trying not to be fearful when encountering an angel is we often do not realize until after the fact we have had an angelic encounter. Recently, my entire family had encountered quick glimpses of various angels standing by one or more of our windows looking in, or somewhere outside of our house just walking around our property. We see them…then we don't see them—it is a mystery. We prayed and dedicated this land and house to the Lord, asking for a release of his assigned angels to guard my family and all who come on the property. We were here about a year before we started seeing glimpses of them. We are now praying God would open our spiritual eyes on a constant basis to see those He has sent to protect and guard us (Psalm 91:11).

Airport Angels

A recent angelic encounter began in the Douglas Charlotte International Airport. I was making every attempt possible to obtain an earlier flight than the one I had booked. I even had my name put down to go standby, but to no avail. While I was waiting for my plane, an older man seated next to me reached over, patted me on the knee and said, "It is ok son, you will arrive in plenty of time."

After introducing myself, I asked what he did for a living. He said, "I am with three others, and we travel all over the earth. You might say the four of us are like special travel agents."

I never gave a second thought to what the older man had said. The only thing on my mind was arriving at my destination on time. A few minutes later the ticket agent informed me I could not fly standby, and I would have to go back and wait for another five hours to get on my previously scheduled flight. With that information, I realized I had ample time on my hands. I wanted a cup of coffee and felt I should offer to buy the older man a cup of coffee as well. I turned to ask him to join me, but he was gone. He was nowhere in sight. That particular area in the airport was not overly crowded, but somehow he had disappeared quickly. I shrugged it off and returned to the assigned departure area and began my wait while sipping on my coffee.

Four hours later, the flight attendant announced my flight was on schedule. I turned to pick up my carry-on luggage and caught a glimpse across the corridor of the same older man who earlier had sat next to me. The next time I looked up, he was standing right next to me. I asked him how he got over to me so fast and where had he gone.

Smiling he said, "I told you I am like a travel agent" and he left it at that. He pointed to the time and departure board and said, "Look, I am on the same flight." The airline attendant announced that all first class passengers were to begin boarding. This older man was the very first person to walk down the walkway to board our flight.

I was in the last group to board. In fact, I was the second from the last to board. As I walked toward my seat, I carefully looked to see if I could spot the older man. After sitting down I looked up and saw him. I had watched him; he was the first one to head down the walkway to board the plane. How was it he was the last to get on? There was nowhere for him to have hidden from my view as I went to my seat. I was puzzled but again I shrugged it off and opened my Bible to read.

When we arrived in Little Rock, it was very late, and I had to change planes. I had to obtain another boarding pass from a different airline to complete my trip.

After I cleared the security area for the second time that day, I found the elevator and went down to the tram area. The area was being remolded and there were no signs posted anywhere to indicate which tram I was to take and where I was to get off.

    I was frustrated. I now had to go back upstairs to find an attendant to ask for directions. I turned towards the elevator, which had closed the moment I cleared its automatic eye. As I turned around there was the same old gent again. This time he was standing right behind me, not one foot away from me. I was so absorbed with trying to find my way around I never considered how he might have gotten there. I had been the only one in the elevator earlier and there were no stairs anywhere in sight, there was only one elevator. No one else was in sight during the time I made my way through security, nor was there anyone with me in the elevator.

    With a big smile the old gentleman said, "You want to get on tram 'B' and get off at tram gate 'D.' Oh, by the way, I am going to be going a lot further than you, but you will do fine, just fine," as he patted me on my shoulder. We both entered the same tram. He never said anything else to me while we were in motion. When the tram door opened at my exit he said, "Take the elevator up to the third level and when the doors open there will be a man standing there waiting for you. He will take you to where your flight gate is, remember, everything will be alright; you'll be just fine."

I stood there for a few moments and watched as the tram door closed and took off. I could see the old man smile and wave back to me as his tram went around the next corner and disappeared out of sight.

It was just like the old man said. At the third floor the elevator door opened and there was a young man standing there waiting for me! As I stepped out of the elevator, he smiled at me and without saying a word, motioned for me to follow him. About five minutes later we rounded a corner and stopped. He pointed to a wide long hallway and then motioned for me to go down the hall. As I started walking away he finally spoke to me saying, "At the end of this hall is where your departure gate is." I looked down the long hallway and then back his way, only to realize he was nowhere around.

Remember, "We are not to forget to entertain strangers, for by so doing some have unwittingly entertained angels" (Hebrews 13:1-2). Again, I was puzzled, tired and yet glad to know which way to go. Several times I wondered where and how all these people had disappeared to so fast? It was a big place with lots of halls and corners to turn, but I finally reached the ticket counter.

After checking in with the ticket agent I sat down, relieved to be at the correct place. All of a sudden, I saw the old man in a vision. He was smiling at me and his words came back to me, "It will be ok" as he patted my arm. At that moment, I almost felt as if I had awakened from a time of sleeping. I began to realize I had an angelic encounter and did not know it.

Partially due to jet lag but mostly due to my stupidity, I found myself repenting again—this time for being so earthly minded and missing the possible opportunity of visiting and gaining more knowledge and insight into the deeper things of God. I had over an hour to wait for the next flight, so I got out my Bible to read for a while. When I laid it on my lap it randomly opened to Zechariah 4. As I read the first verse, chills ran throughout my entire body.

"Now the angel who talked with me came back and wakened me, as a man who is wakened out of his sleep" (Zechariah 4:1).

Boy, oh boy, oh boy, when I blow it, I really blow it! I spent the short trip on the airplane repenting for the spiritual condition of the eyes of my heart.

Bible Reading

My goal was to read 20 chapters a day from my Bible, which took approximately four hours including coffee refills. I was on target with my goal when I received a divine interruption by a heavenly messenger. An angel appeared in a dream and said, "Duane, the Lord wants you to study three chapters a day from out of His word instead of reading 20 chapters."

After breakfast, I began my new journey of Bible study. To my surprise, it requires the same amount of time to study three chapters as compared to reading twenty chapters.

"Study to shew thyself approved unto God, a workman that needeth not to be ashamed, rightly dividing the word of truth" (2 Timothy 2:15).

As I read my Bible, I always have a pen and pad in hand, and I always read just loud enough so I may hear what I am reading, which is writing the word of God on my heart. Faith comes by hearing and hearing by the word of God. As I hear the word of God coming from my own lips, I get prophetic revelation.

One of the reasons I read my Bible aloud as I study is because it takes one hundred positive affirmations to cancel out one negative statement. We need to counteract all doubt and unbelief with the word of God. Over the years, I have learned it is best to read my Bible just before going to bed at night. As I sleep the Holy Spirit puts emphasis on whatever I have read.

Let not [words of] mercy and truth forsake you; Bind them around your neck, [say them aloud and you will] **write them on the tablet of your heart**, and so find favor and high esteem in the sight of God and man (Proverbs 3:3, 4).

A Prophetic Token

One afternoon my wife and I were relaxing on our front porch nursing two of those fancy coffees with the whip cream and chocolate drizzled all over the top. Our entertainment was watching our daughter do a Bible skit.

Our daughter had been complaining for the third straight day that God never gave her any prophetic tokens like the ones He gave me. This particular afternoon she was walking around our front yard with my walking stick when I said to her, "Throw down that rod like Moses did and it will turn into a snake" (Exodus 7).

About that same time she looked up, smiled at me sarcastically while sporting a big fake smile as she let my walking stick fall from her hand onto the ground and bounce several times. When the walking stick hit the ground, a five foot snake rushed out from under a nearby bush and began hissing and striking at her. She quickly jumped backwards and ran to the porch for safety. The snake became so aggressive, I had to kill it.

After the entire event was over, I smiled at my daughter and said, "Now you can quit complaining. You have just received your prophetic token for the week."

Her response was, "Daddy, I do not want any of those prophetic things happening to me or around me. No thank you, Amen." She is not so quick to complain about not receiving prophetic tokens now.

15 Pounds in 15 Days

While ministering in Ontario, Canada I asked a young woman to come down front to receive prophetic ministry. The Holy Spirit revealed she was depressed, discouraged, and anxious about her life. I said, "Young woman, the Holy Spirit is going to give you a token of the Father's love. Go home and weigh yourself and write it down on your calendar. You will lose 15 pounds in 15 days."

Five months later, we were ministering at the same church when I asked the same woman to come down and give a testimony. She said, "That day I went home and weighed, and ten days later I weighted again and discovered that I had lost 10 pounds, but I forgot to weight again at the end of the fifteen days." Then she said, "Oh, all of my clothes are still really loose on me."

As she was walking back to her seat I stopped her and said, "Young woman, God is not through with you yet. You will lose another 15 pounds in 15 days" (Romans 10:17).

To be full or to be a Fool

This came for me personally in a vision. I was taking steps to trim down and lose weight and at the same time tone my muscles. I do not know if I will ever again reach my wedding weight, but I am trying. A faceless man (the Holy Spirit) appeared to me and said, "Anyone who eats until they are full is a Fool."

As he spoke, I kept tilting my head in various directions to see if I could see what he looked like but was unable to get a clear image of his face other than just an outline. After this encounter, conviction came and I have become serious about eating healthier foods. So far, I have been losing about one–half pound every five days (Proverbs 23:3).

A Weekly Meeting

While living in Missouri, I was instructed by the Holy Spirit to give a man a white candle, and while he held the candle I was to light it. I was at a friend's home and finally after looking around in the kitchen, I was able to find a small stub of a white candle, so it had to do. I asked the man to hold the candle as I lit it. As he was holding it, I read Revelation 1:20 over the man.

"The mystery of the seven stars which you saw in My right hand, and the seven golden lamp stands: The seven stars are the angels of the seven churches, and the seven lamp stands (candles) which you saw are the seven churches" (Revelation 1:20)

Stars are angels; ministers also represent angels. The white candle represented a church. That was his commissioning to start a meeting. The last I heard, he had begun a weekly men's meeting at a neighborhood restaurant.

Some Clarity

It was the second year my house was for sale. I was just about to give up and keep the house when I heard the Holy Spirit say, "Change your prayer." Later that evening I was led to ask God to give a token to the person who was to buy my house (instead of giving me a token so my house would sell).

"Ask thee a sign of the Lord thy God; ask it either in the depth, or in the height above" (Isaiah 7:11).

Two weeks later a woman knocked on my front door and said, "I want to buy your house, how much do you want for it?" After we agreed on a price, I asked why she chose my house instead of another.

She told me I had seven fruit trees in my back yard and all seven trees had seven pieces of fruit on each of them, and she felt that was God's sign to her to buy my house.

That one instance has changed the way I pray and minister to this day. I now ask God to give tokens to confirm His will for others. Since that day, I have declared prophetic tokens over thousands of people.

The number seven means perfection, rest, sanctification, and more than enough. God has seven redemptive names and the seventh commandment "Do not commit adultery." In fact, I have written a handbook, which covers Bible numbers.

Original or Counterfeit

God is the creator of everything; Satan only counterfeits or duplicates what God has already created. Satan does not have the ability to create anything on his own. As an example, tattoos are the counterfeit of what God has done in His creation.

"You shall not make any cuttings in your flesh for the dead, nor tattoo any marks on you: I am the Lord" (Leviticus 19:28).

I had a vision of a relative lying on his stomach next to a swimming pool sunbathing. In the vision, the relative had two and one third columns of blue writing on his back. The writing was similar to the following, but it was not in English, therefore I could not read it.

The tattooed writing was similar to this style and size. The font was a fancy script.

When I saw the writing, I was puzzled because I knew this relative disliked any form of a tattoo. I pondered the vision for several weeks before the Lord gave me one word, "Destiny," concerning the tattoo or spiritual marks. The tattoo was not visible to the naked eye; I saw it by the spiritual eyes of my heart.

For the past 15 years, I have often wondered what the writing said since the man was not a Christian and died in his sins. Could the writing have been his spiritual destiny he never attempted or chose to yield too?

Several years ago, the Holy Spirit revealed to me what the tattoo represented. God spiritually marks everyone prior to their birth. At the same time, many others who became Christians have been marked with the ink of the **writer's inkhorn**. This particular group of people will declare the end time decrees of God. This marking is in the spiritual realm rather than the physical or natural realm.

"...One man among them was clothed with linen and had a **writer's inkhorn** at his side ... Moreover, the Lord said to him, Go through the midst of the city, through the midst of Jerusalem, and **put a mark on the foreheads of the men** (and women) who sigh and cry over all the abominations,..." (Ezekiel 9:2-11).

Unfortunately, there will be a countless number of people during the end of this age who will freely accept the devil's counterfeit mark, or the number of his mark—

666. Without the devil's mark no one will not be able to buy, sell, or trade. The worldwide economic mark will be on the right hand or the forehead.

"The antichrist will causes all, both small and great, rich and poor, free and slave, **to receive a mark** on their right hand or on their foreheads ..." (Revelation 13:16-17; and chapters 14, 15, 16, 19, 20).

The devil's mark is the counterfeit to the mark of God seen in Ezekiel 9. The devil's mark will always be in the natural realm and will be similar to a tattoo in its appearance. **The mark of God will always be in the spiritual realm and NOT visible to the naked eye.**

I have given this partial teaching to make my readers aware that God has spiritually marked everyone on planet earth. His markings are always for the good; they are never for any form of evil. Man has a free will and has the freedom to follow and obey God or reject Him and follow Satan who is the god of this world.

If God gave you the blueprints to build you a beautiful house and when the time came to begin building, you rejected His plans and designed your own house, what outcome do you expect? You will NOT hear well done my good and faithful servant. I do not know exactly what you will hear but it will probably not be very pleasing (Matthew 25:14-30).

Many times I have seen spiritual marks and / or writings on people. These marks vary in color and size. Normally they are in a language I cannot read. Each time the Lord has always provided me with the interpretation of these marks and writings by the gift of discerning of spirits (1 Corinthians 12:10). In the past, I have seen marks and writings on people's arms, hands, fingers, feet, legs, backs, shoulders, necks and faces.

The majority of the time the marks are on the hands and fingers. When I am seeking a word for a person, I have asked them to hold out their hands. When I do this, **"I am Not Reading Their Palms,"** I am looking for spiritual colors or marks—mostly on their fingers. At times I may have them place their hands on mine (palm to palm) and then I ask the Holy Spirit to illuminate their gifts and calling. Sometimes when I do this, there has been warmth or an electrical shock flowing into one or more of their fingers. The right hand represents blessings and the left hand ministry.

When I see spiritual marks on the feet, I know that person has a higher level of power and authority then most people to crush the head of Satan (Romans 16:20). When I see spiritual writings on a person's jaw that tells me their call is in the area of singing, teaching and or public speaking.

Please understand. God does not reveal such spiritual marks or writings on everyone I meet or see. In fact, the majority of the time I operate in word of knowledge, word of wisdom, prophecy, the discerning of spirits, or the gift of discernment (1 Corinthians 12:8-10; Philippians 1:9). I will only ask to see a person's hands as a last option. A large portion of the body of Christ has not matured and developed their spiritual discernment to a level of trusting and knowing that God is a good God and that He is the author of all things.

To my dismay, in the past I have asked to see a person's hands only to later find out they were an immature Christian and unable to receive or accept this level of ministry.

> "For though by this time you ought to be teachers, you need someone to teach you again the first principles of the oracles of God; and you have come to need milk and not solid food. **For everyone who partakes only of milk is unskilled in the word of righteousness, for he is a babe. But solid food belongs to those who are of full age, that is, those who by reason of use have their senses exercised to discern both good and evil**" (Hebrews 5:12-14).

I also feel the need to give a deeper explanation concerning tokens. A token is nothing more than a point of contact designed to help build a person's faith in the word of God. Many who receive a prophetic word do not know what to do with the prophetic word and at times do not really believe the prophetic will come to pass in their lives.

If the prophetic word of God to a person is, "The devil is leaving your house, and the Lord is going to save everyone who enters into your house this summer," at first, they may think "Wow that is great," but as time goes by, their faith dwindles if they are not rooted and grounded in the word of God.

Therefore, at times the Lord will give a token to keep their spiritual eyes of faith focused on His personal prophetic word to them. The token may be for them to take a red cord and tie it around the front door's doorknob and all who enter in through that door will believe on the Lord Jesus Christ as their personal savior and receive salvation (Joshua 2:18, 21; Acts 16:31). The prophetic word did not say they would believe that day, week, month or even that year. However, I have heard of many who believed and received salvation during that particular season.

A token has no power in itself, nor can a token save a person. A token and a fleece are opposites of each other. Men ask God for a fleece because of their unbelief. God initiates tokens to build a person's faith. As I said earlier, a token is nothing more than a point of contact designed to help build a person's faith in the word of God. It will help keep you in remembrance of the prophetic word, which God has released to you.

Some of the prophetic tokens that God has told me to release to His body were such things as follows: One time the Holy Spirit told me to tell a person not to cut or trim her hair for forty days. This action increased the anointing of God upon that person's life (Judges 16:22). After complying with the word, one individual said a holy boldness came upon her, which enabled her to share the gospel of Jesus Christ with everyone she met.

Once, by the leading of the Lord, I told a person to anoint their feet with oil every night for three days so they would have a walk of good success (3 John 2). The following week they began a new career without the usual red tape everyone else who was also applying for the same opportunity had to deal with. In the past, the red tape had hindered their education and career change, but this time it was as if the red tape held everyone else back and opened the door for them to begin entering into their destiny. In addition, they received a monthly living expense account and a substantial bonus for starting that same week.

By the leading of the Lord, I have given out countless prayer cloths to people. Many received miracles such as breaking the curse of barrenness, diseases left, evil spirits came out of people, more than once the anointing stopped an inevitable miscarriage, and one man came back to life after having an allergic reaction to the medicine he received while in a hospital. Cloth can easily carry the anointing of the Holy Spirit (Matthew 9:20; 14:36; Mark 6:56; Acts 19:11, 12).

On one occasion, by the leading of the Lord I gave a young man a sandwich made of wheat bread and honey butter. A week later, he rededicated his life to Christ and is now attending church (1 Samuel 14:27).

One time I heard the Holy Spirit say for me to give a man a pair of my shoes. That same week the man began walking two miles one way to a church near his house. Eventually he believed the preached word and made a profession of faith.

While having lunch one Sunday, by the leading of the Lord, I told our waiter God loved her and was in the process of changing her name. She gave me a strange look and said, "I like my name." Weeks later, she met a

Christian man, fell in love and they were married a short time later. When she was single, she was Miss. Lonely but now she is married and is Mrs. Joyful (not her real names). Her last name changed when she married (Genesis 17; 32; Hebrews 13:4).

At various times during the past thirty years, by the leading of the Lord, I told different people they were to drink a large glass of water; others were instructed to drink a large glass of milk, and a few were told to drink a large glass of buttermilk as they read their Bible. This is similar to priming a water pump, except it is in the spiritual realm drawing out living water from the word of life. Each of these tokens birthed a supernatural hunger and thirst for the word of God in the man or woman who acted in accordance with the prophetic token (Revelation 22:17).

Once I called a man out and told him God had heard his request to hear with greater spiritual clarity. As a token his ears were going to begin running wax. Later that summer I saw that same man and he reported his ears ran wax for three days after he received the prophetic word.

The Holy Spirit led me to tell one man to anoint his ears with olive oil before reading his bible and he would begin to grow in revelational faith. The next time we met, he was walking on cloud nine with faith and greater understanding (Proverbs 23:23; Romans 10:17).

One time when I lived in Florida, I was walking past a group of Spirit filled believers leaving a coffee shop.

The Holy Spirit told me to stop and ask each of them to call out the names of five unsaved family members (five is the number of God's unmerited grace). I then told them everyone they named would receive salvation before the person's next birthday. I gave them all a business card and asked for testimonies about what God did. Several months passed before I began receiving reports of salvations of the names they had lifted up (Acts 16:31).

Another time the Holy Spirit revealed I was to tell a pastor how to deal with the lukewarm believers in his church. At one time, these believers were on fire for the gospel of Christ but it dwindled to nought. "Tell him to anoint each member's forehead with the sign of the cross using salt water and then sprinkle a little raw salt on the tip of their tongues." Over a period of several weeks, those who came down to reactivate the salt covenant once again became the salt of the earth (Luke 9:49, 50). During the following weeks, many of his parishioners once again began witnessing for Jesus Christ.

There are times when the Holy Spirit instructs me to tell an individual to do a prophetic action and that produces a higher level of faith. Their action is nothing more than a point of contact. Many times the individual moves into a higher level of the prophetic and that produces the desired results they are in need of.

At times, I have come under major criticism because of the prophetic tokens I have given out over the years. People ask, "Do you really know if this stuff is from God?" To that question, I suggest they read about the prophet who threw a bowl of salt into the bitter waters, which healed the waters to this day (2Kings 2:20) or when he threw a wooden limb into the lake to make an iron ax head float (2Kings 6:5). I do not know a believer who has not heard about Elijah instructing the widow at Zarephath to make him a little cake first and then her house would not starve (1Kings 17:10). The prophet Ezekiel ate bread by measure once God told him to build a miniature wall and then make a mock siege against it signifying a future attack (Ezekiel 4). One prophet was told to walk bare foot and naked (without his prophets mantle) for a certain length of time (Isaiah 20:20). Another prophet was to marry the town whore and to name their children after the judgments of God (Hosea). Jesus washed the disciple's feet, which was a prophetic token of a future inward action (John 13).

    I read in my Bible the "Lord God does not change neither is there a shadow of His turning." In addition "If anyone lacks wisdom, let him ask of God, who giveth to everyone liberally, and upbraideth not; and it shall be given them. However, let him ask in faith, nothing wavering...For every good gift and every perfect gift is from above, and cometh down from the Father of lights with whom is no variableness, neither shadow of turning" (Malachi 3:6; James 1:5-6, 17). Godly blessings are from God!

    I cannot stress enough that **I Do Not Ask for Tokens at My Own Choosing**. Only when I have received instructions from the Holy Spirit will I do such. It is His gifts, tokens of His ministry, and it is His manifested glory given to Jesus through such events.

Levitation

A man asked me if God could help him with his balance and walk. He was constantly tripping, falling and stumbling on a weekly basis; often he physically injured himself from falling. His doctor could not find any medical reason for his problem but did suggest that he should get his vision checked. Later his eye doctor also gave him a clean bill of health.

At one time, I had this same problem in my life so I knew exactly what his problem was. After canceling "The Spirit of Levitation" his balance and walk came into alignment. No longer was he tripping, falling and stumbling. In fact, the last time we spoke he had not tripped, fallen or stumbled for over a year.

"Father God by your Sons blood and cross I cancel all tripping, falling and stumbling that comes from the spirit of Levitation against everyone who is reading this book right now in Jesus name Amen.

Candles

We accompanied a Christian friend to the home of a family in need of prophetic ministry. After entering the couple's home, they insisted on visiting with us about their geographic location, unemployment, and their children. I tried to tell them I did not want to hear anything concerning their family or their situation—I would rather hear from the Holy Spirit than from a human. When the sun began to set, Mrs. Anxious (not her real name) gathered a large number of white candles, placed them around the room and carefully lit each one. When she did this, I remembered what she said concerning their recent financial losses and thought she was trying to save electricity.

I bowed my head and waited for the Lord, but saw nothing. About thirty minutes later, I told them the Lord had not revealed anything to me concerning their family. I closed with a generic prayer asking God to send His Holy Spirit to make their entire family holy in total obedience to His word, will and way.

Several months later, we visited a good friend, Barbara C., who is a powerful intercessor. As we all waited before the Lord, our friend Barbara began to pray and immediately I had an open vision.

In the vision, I saw Mrs. Anxious, her living room, and the white candles lit all around the room. I then heard the Lord say, "You were in the house of a spiritualist (white witchcraft)." I immediately fell on my face and repented for even being there.

Then the Lord said something that surprised me. "You needed to learn firsthand what it is you are fighting so you will know when to fight" (Deuteronomy 18:10-13).

Snow Angels

It was February when we arrived with the final load in Arkansas. It was below freezing with ice on the highway. We arrived in Texarkana at 8 p.m. and I became aware of the huge chunks of ice hanging from the running boards and under the fender wells. My wife had been waiting all day in our newly painted house for the moving van and was unaware it had turned back due to bad weather. I was unaware of this information also and pressed forward to meet up with everyone.

It was the third hour of a one hour trip. We were the only vehicles on the road after we left Texarkana, Texas. It was eerily silent and at times the only thing we could hear was the purr of the engine. My son had disconnected the radio so we had no weather information, and that was probably the hand of God working on our behalf keeping fear away.

Josh mentioned that the last twenty miles were the most dangerous with thirty foot drop offs leading down into a creek on both sides of the road, and asked, "What are we going to do?"

"Pray my son, pray, pray, pray. We are going to pray that God will send two angels ahead of us to clear the snow off the road so we will see where we are driving and not run off the road and kill ourselves."

A few minutes later, we saw the sign indicating our turn off was two miles ahead. As we rounded a corner, I could see two sets of headlights in the far distance coming towards us. Twenty minutes later we were 1/8 of a mile from our turn off when we identified two approaching vehicles—both were tractor-trailers. They were driving as slow as we were.

All three vehicles reached the road that intersected with the highway at the same time. I was glad the two tractor-trailers turned ahead of us going in our direction.

Josh said, "this is cool, two angels showed up just as we had asked for in prayer."

I pulled in behind the second semi and did my best to stay as close as possible to it the entire trip. The next twenty miles passed faster than I imagined. The blowing snow worsened as soon as we turned and followed the tractor–trailers. At one point the snow and sleet had begun to blow so badly I had to stay five feet behind the tractor–trailers.

Finally, we were within a mile of our turn off which was a side road into our driveway. We waved and thanked God as the tractor–trailers kept going past our turn off. The road in front of our house was the same road the tractor–trailers would intersect with and was only 200 yards beyond our house. The snow and sleet had stopped and we could see a white blanket of snow on the roadway from the streetlights beaming into the darkness. The two semis had disappeared into thin air—they were nowhere in sight. They had to either take a left turn at the intersection, which would have led them directly in front of our house or they would have had to take a right turn, which would have taken them through town. There were no tire tracks in either direction in the 6 inches of fresh snow that blanketed the roadway. The two tractor–trailers were nowhere in sight in either direction nor could we hear the rumble of their exhaust.

My son was dumbfounded. We were both glad to be home and my wife's prayers had been answered. God safely delivered us into her arms. "For God will order His angels to protect you wherever you go" (Psalm 91:11).

God is waiting for His children to ask Him for help. Too often, we ask but in most cases, we ask with our own strategy in mind. God wants to reveal Himself as our deliver, our provider for everything. Remember we must ask God in faith, not doubting for he that wavereth is like a wave of the sea driven with the wind and tossed (James 1:6).

The Hot Tub Adventure

We had just moved into an apartment in Springfield, and my wife had taken an evening job at the hospital, which left my daughter and me to fend for ourselves five evenings a week. I was excited about trying out the hot tub and my four–year–old daughter was eager to go for a swim. By sunset, the temperature had dropped down just enough to produce a fine steam above the hot tub bubbles. As I was enjoying a time of relaxing in the hot tub my daughter ran over and sat down on the edge, dangling her feet in the steaming bubbles. Looking up she said, "Daddy who are those men up there in the sky wearing white dresses?"

Glancing upwards, I saw that the heavens had opened up and a group of angels was looking down on the earth. "Those are angels, honey."

"Ok daddy" was her response as she ran over and jumped back into the swimming pool. The following morning as I sat on my patio reading my Bible, she came out to say good morning and immediately said, "Oh Daddy, look there are those men again in white dresses." I glanced upwards just in time to see the open heavens close up and I never saw the angels again.

As the weeks passed by, we created a new family tradition. Every evening my daughter would swim and I would soak in the hot tub. We both met others and developed light friendships with our new neighbors.

I was impressed with one man in particular who had just celebrated his fifteenth year as a Christian (The number 15 represents having the ability to hear what the Holy Spirit is saying; Jesus said 15 times, let he who has ears to hear let him hear...). The two of us spent several hours a week talking about the Bible. I soon realized this young man was extremely knowledgeable about the scriptures. He told me how he had tried countless times to do a home group or a Bible study only to have no one show up. As the weeks and conversations continued, I learned he had never received water baptism. Therefore, I began teaching him on the benefits and blessings of water baptism.

I made the explanation of water baptism as simple as possible. Water baptism is our part of the signing of the covenant. Try purchasing a vehicle and attempt to leave the bank or dealership without signing the contract (It Will Not Happen). You do not own the vehicle until you sign on the dotted line. You could say that water baptism is our signing on the dotted line. We continued to meet and talk on the topic for the remainder of the week. I personally believe that water baptism will help equip us to stand in the gap and make up the hedge. Following the example that Christ gave us in receiving water baptism imparts an inward knowing of obedience into the life of the believer.

I really feel some clarification on the above statement is needed. I do not believe one has to be water baptized to receive salvation. Jesus told the thief on the cross "Verily, verily I say unto thee, today shalt thou be with me in paradise" (Luke 23:43). When the thief believed Jesus was the Son of God his name went into the Lambs Book of Life. Water baptism was not and is still not a requirement to receive salvation. Water baptism symbolically represents cutting off the sin nature. John the Baptist told everyone who received water baptism they should bear fruits worthy of repentance. Water baptism is an outward sign of an inward work (1 Corinthians 15:46).

One Saturday afternoon, the young man stopped by the hot tub wearing dress slacks, a polo shirt, and wingtips. He was a few minutes ahead of his schedule and had time to visit. From out of the blue, he asked if I would baptize him. I gladly said yes. After he went and changed clothes, I gave him the choice of the hot tub or the swimming pool. To my surprise, he kicked off his shoes, jumped into the hot tub, and said, "Let's do it." I led him through a prayer of rededication and then put him under. When he came up out of the water, he commented that his entire body felt electrified. I could hear him praising God all the way around the corner as he went to change clothes.

I became alarmed the following week because I did not see the young man nor had anyone else who knew of our visits and the water baptism. Two months passed before I heard anything at all. One evening he just showed up at the hot tub and gave an awesome report.

The day after receiving water baptism, he began leading a men's Bible study at his work place. Two weeks later, several people contacted him and asked if they could come to his home group, asking when and where it met. I do not remember all of the particulars but he was now teaching at three home groups a week plus the Bible study at his work place on Saturday mornings. Praise God!

Did water baptism open up the blessings of God? I personally believe it did. I wonder how many of my readers have never been water baptized? What is God waiting to release to you when you obey and are water baptized?

Everywhere I speak, I do my best to repeat this story. Over the past years, I have discovered there are many believers who have never received water baptism. If you want Romans 12:1, 2 to come alive in your life, make sure you have been water baptized.

Many have only been christened or sprinkled as children. If you are one of those, you may want to pray about taking the big plunge and receive submersion baptism. Remember water baptism is our signing on the dotted line. Christening, sprinkling and water baptism will not save a person nor will it get anyone into heaven. Water baptism is the outward example of an inward work of the Holy Spirit. It is our obedience and following our Lord and Savior Jesus Christ in baptismal waters as He did (Matthew 3:13-17; Mark 1:9, 10; Luke 3:21, 22; John

1:29-34). Remember partial obedience is total disobedience.

A Name Change

During the spring of 2009, I had been studying scriptures concerning God changing the names of different people in the Bible. God changed Abram's name to Abraham and Sari's name to Sarah (Genesis 17). God changed Jacob's name to Israel (Genesis 32). Jesus changed Simon's name to Peter although Peter was his given name (Matthew 16). Saul had his name changed to Paul (Acts 13).

We have a friend, Ann, who had a visitation from Jesus. Before the visitation was over, Jesus added the letter "a" after her given name, Ann changing it to Anna. Over the past thirty years, I have heard other similar stories. Each time I wondered about the significance of God changing a person's name.

I shared my thoughts with my wife on my study of names and she commented that a woman's last name changes when she marries. At least that was the way it was at one time. When the woman takes on her husband's last name, she is publicly identifying herself as one with him.

For several days, as I pondered everything concerning God changing or altering an individual's name, I toyed with the idea of adding various letters to my existing name. Thank God He did not do that as they all sound like a person from another planet.

Recently my wife and I heard of a prophet holding meetings just ten miles from where we lived. We decided to venture over and check it out. I want to explain why I chose to go. I really enjoy watching and listening to good prophetic teaching and preaching and I enjoy watching them operate in their supernatural gifts and calling. Probably the most important reason was; I wanted my youngest daughter to see a ministry that moved in signs, wonders and miracles—"The Real Deal"—and that was exactly what happened. What I mean by "The Real Deal" is that there were no bells and whistles or fluff and puffed up stuff going on. In plain simple words "No Gimmicks."

Several times I was personally distracted from watching and listening to the prophet because I was watching my daughter's expressions of excitement and joy. She was awestruck for the first three nights. Most of the time she was on the edge of her seat in total amazement. For a moment, I thought she was going to jump through the ceiling when we all saw a deformed leg grow out. The bone between the knee and ankle was several inches shorter than the man's other leg. In plain view of everyone present, his leg grew out with no one touching him. He left the meeting that evening in his stocking feet. It was impossible for him to wear his elevated shoe and walk evenly. His pants leg was even several inches shorter and did not cover the new portion of his leg that God had healed.

The prophet did not know anything about me or my family when he called me up front and said, "Donald, the Lord is going to take 40 pounds off of you in 40 days."

Then he told me several other things God was doing in my life. I corrected him each time he called me Donald. I told him four times my name was Duane not Donald. After I sat back down, my wife Karah punched me in the shoulder and asked, "What is your first name?" I had to think for a few moments before I said, "It is Donald! Why didn't I remember that?" After years of using my middle name, I never answered to the name of Donald. However, God called me "Donald" that night.

The second night of the meeting, the prophet walked past where I was seated and paused for a moment and asked, "Have you learned your name is Donald yet?" He smiled and went on up to the platform.

The third night we attended the meeting the prophet walked over to where I was seated and asked, "Donald have you realized yet that God has changed your name and you are to be called Donald from now on? God does not want you to use your middle name, Duane, any longer. From now on, Donald is the name you are to use. The Lord says that He is changing your character, nature, and name. You are to use the name you were given at birth." Donald means "Ruler and some other good stuff! Look it up!" he said, as he walked off.

I am a firm believer you must act on whatever you truly believe. That night after we arrived home, I went in and changed the automatic signature on my email to print Donald. I opened about fifty documents that contained my middle name Duane and did a 'find and replace' with my corrected name Donald. This was the beginning of my act of faith to the prophetic word. Faith without works is dead (James 2:22). The following Monday when I took the trash out to the curb, I happened to look in the mailbox. We do not receive mail at our home address. We use a post office box because it is more convenient for us and offers a greater level of security. I was surprised to find two pieces of mail had arrived both addressed to Donald Young. The words of two or three witnesses will establish a matter (Deuteronomy 19:15; 2 Corinthians 13:1). The number two also has a spiritual significance. The number two (2) in scripture is the number for witnesses.

I am the type of individual who does not just completely accept anything a person says to me. I did believe the prophetic word concerning my name change, but I still took the entire situation back to God in prayer. I specifically asked God if this was true concerning my name change to send me a second witness. Two days later my daughter happened to check the mailbox and again there were two pieces of mail addressed to Donald Young, no middle name or initial. The testimony of two men is true (John 8:17). I had my two witnesses.

I have wrestled with the idea of writing a book like this one for over ten years. Every time I began to write, I felt I was being too prideful. A minister told me I was struggling with misdirected humility not pride. He pointed out every time I told about a prophetic occurrence in my life I always used it as a teaching tool for others. When the Lord changed my name, he began changing my character and nature. Since I have been using my given name, Donald, the feeling of pride left and I actually enjoyed sharing my encounters especially when I am able to teach others.

My deepest desire is for you, my reader, to step out of your boat and walk on the water of the supernatural. Give God an opportunity to do something supernatural in your life. You will never encounter God in a supernatural way unless you are willing to risk your time, talents, treasures and reputation. Do not worry what others may or may not think and say about you. Go for it. God is waiting to pour out His blessing over you and your ministry. Without faith it is impossible to please God, for faith without works is dead. Remember, when you want something you have never had you have to do something you have never done. You will only possess what you are passionately pursuing.

Mark 2:22

The same year I became a radical believer the Lord told me my walk with Him would always have a double witness. In other words, everything God tells me to do will always have two witnesses. One of the witnesses could be a vision, a prophetic word, a dream, etc... The second witness will always come from the scriptures. If scripture does not confirm what He has told me, I wait for further instructions.

Shortly after the first week of 2010, I began to feel a strong urge to draw aside and fast. While in prayer, I began asking God how long He wanted me to fast. I never received a reply. Therefore, I kept asking. Each week I would increase the number of days I was willing to fast and I still did not get a response from the throne room. On Monday, February 22, I lifted up a particular number of days I was willing to fast just as I had for weeks prior. Before I could say Amen, I heard the Holy Spirit say Mark 2:22:

"No one puts new wine into old wineskins; or else the new wine bursts the wineskins, the wine is spilled, and the wineskins are ruined. But new wine must be put into new wineskins."

This was the double confirmation from God concerning my prayer request to fast for a certain length of days. My answer came on February 22, which is the second month of the year and the twenty-second day (2, 22) and the scripture reference was (Mark 2:22).

God loves us to ask for confirmations. Do not be bashful about asking Him to repeat Himself.

"Ask a sign for yourself from the Lord your God; ask it either in the depth or in the height above" (Isaiah 7:11).

A Knife

March began as a typical month, but it soon escalated to far more than I could imagine. I had promised my wife that I would do some minor repairs while she went to town. I had not paid attention to the time as I had been pressing into the things of God to obtain a fresh touch. I paused for a few minutes, knelt down, and repented for any form of slothfulness that might have hindered any part of my walk with Him. I felt a peace and the presence of God come into the room. For nearly an hour, the overwhelming sensation of God's presence was so strong I nearly forgot to do the repairs I had promised my wife I would take care of.

When I realized she would be home any minute, I rushed out to the garage with an inward joy flowing out of my spirit. I had not felt that awesome in a long time.

I entered the garage through a service door and immediately flipped on the lights that were on a cinder block wall that firmly holds the switch box and metal conduit pipe in place. The week before I had wedged a Stanley dry wall saw—knife with a ten inch double-sided blade with an extremely sharp point between the metal conduit and the cinder block wall.

I gathered the tools and parts I would need and headed back into the house. Approximately ten feet from the service door, I looked down towards the floor long enough to rethink the repair job. When I looked back up, I saw the Stanley dry wall knife flying through the air towards my chest. The knife stopped in midair in front of my heart area and fell to the floor. Thank God He gives His angels charge over those who believe in His name (Psalm 91:11).

After I commanded the enemy to leave my property, I took time out to thank God. When my wife arrived, I showed her the knife and told her the story. She said, "Honey you do know that we went to a higher level in the prophetic last month. It only makes sense the attacks have also gone to a higher level. A greater level of the anointing will encounter higher devils. We cast out demons but we wrestle against principalities" (Mark 16:17; Ephesians 6:12).

The Day of Atonement
September 27th @6pm through September 28 @ 6pm, 2009

September 28th at 8 a.m., I was awakened by an angel standing next to my bed playing a violin. The music coming from the violin as well as the angel's voice was extremely sad. The angel was crying so intently he had saturated his shirt from the stream of tears that ran down both cheeks. He was singing, "America, America, God shed His grace on thee…"

I became overwhelmed as I listened to the music and the words of the song the angel sang. It was discouraging and I also began to cry. The visitation lasted several minutes.

I am aware that the number eight refers to "New Beginnings." I believe the Church has begun a New Beginning, which will produce a higher level of purity and righteousness. Without righteousness no man will see God (Matthew 5:20).

"For the time is come that judgment must begin at the house of God: and if it first begin at us, what shall the end be of them that obey not the gospel of God? And if the righteous scarcely be saved, where shall the ungodly and the sinner appear" (1stPeter 4:17-18)?

A Word for You

"Hope deferred makes the heart sick: but when the desire cometh, it is a tree of life." Know this says the Lord God; love is your spiritual compass. It will direct you into every supernatural blessing that is awaiting you. "Come, learn of me." I know your heart and your deepest desires. These very desires will catapult you into the place of your destiny. Do not give up, nor give in. At times, you will find yourself in the fires of testing and afterwards you will find yourself submerged in the living water of life. Just as a battle-ax obtains its strength between the fire and the water, so shall your faith find strength! "Remember, prayers that are not prayed, are never answered.'"

A Final Attempt

This is my final attempt to make sure that your name is in the Lamb's book of Life. You have now read pages containing words that told you a little about my life. You have learned a few things about my family, my childhood, about what I like and dislike, and whom I enjoy, and where I enjoy going. Although we have never met, you now know something about me. When you meet others who have read this book, both of you will have the wisdom contained in these pages in common. Although you and the other person will know a little something about me, you still have never met me.

Unfortunately, the vast majority of people are in this very same scenario. They go to church and read their Bible, give tithes and offerings but they only know about

God. They have read about the author of life. They know some of what the Bible says about God. They have read about His family and His friends. They may even know what He likes and dislikes. What they have is an accumulation of information compiled over time.

Jesus gave the human race a major warning that separates those who know about Him from those who are in relationship with Him. At the Final Judgment, thousands will walk up to Jesus and say, "Master, we preached Your word, and we cast out demons, we went to church and read our Bible, we gave tithes and offerings to our God sponsored projects which had everyone excited."

At that moment Jesus is going to say, "Depart from Me I Never Knew You. Everything you did was to make yourself look good or feel important. You do not impress Me one bit. You Will Not Spend Eternity with Me" (Matthew 7:22, 23).

My dear friends, please do not settle for knowing about Jesus the Christ. It is time for you to meet Him personally. Get off by yourself and spend some time repenting aloud your sins. You will not remember all your sins but the Holy Spirit will prompt you in what to say. God will forgive you if you will ask Him. Tell Him you do not know what to do but to call on His name. Ask Jesus Christ into your heart. Tell Him to do anything He needs to do in your life to make sure you are in a correct relationship with Him for all eternity.

"Father God, I ask that you will reach down from your throne of grace, mercy and compassion. I ask that you will physically touch the individual who is calling on you for eternal salvation. Help them enter into a lifelong relationship with Jesus on a daily basis. I ask that Jesus the Christ will supernaturally reveal Himself to them in a way that will reassure them of His presence in their lives for eternity. Thank you Father God for Your promise that says, 'You will never leave us nor forsake us.'"

Prayer Request

We take prayer very seriously. Please feel free to mail or e-mail (NewBeginningsSOS@gmail.com) your prayer request for us to join you in a prayer of agreement for your need.

"Again I say unto you, that if two of you shall agree on earth as touching anything that they shall ask, it shall be done for them of my Father which is in heaven. For where two or three are gathered together in my name, there am I in the midst of them" (Matthew 18:19-20).

"Know Those Who Labor Among You"
1 Thessalonians 5:12

Donald and Karah are radical Holy Spirit filled Christians in love with Jesus. They both are graduates from Christian International School of Theology as licensed and ordained ministers. They were co-pastors in South Texas, and later planted two prophetic Schools of the Spirit. They spent six years with Morning Star Ministries of Charlotte, North Carolina as prophetic team leaders, training others to minister in their gift and calling. Both were pastors with United Methodist Churches in Missouri and Florida.

Karah is a former president of Woman's Aglow in Fort Mill, South Carolina. One of Karah's gifts to the body of Christ is her ability to teach and stir up the gifts in others, while imparting the supernatural power to become an over comer in all areas of everyday practical life. God has used her to heal the wounded and broken hearted. The gift and anointing that God has given Karah have a unique ability to bring supernatural healing and restoration.

They have one daughter who ministers in song, and prophecy. Her singing often opens the heavens allowing a free flow of the Holy Spirit for all present.

Donald and Karah's marriage was a sovereign move of God that was prophesied, confirmed with signs, wonders, and two angelic visitations.

They continually teach and preach the uncompromised Word of God with a message of hope and restoration. They have activated believers from all over the North American continent in the Prophetic and in How to Hear the Voice of God for themselves—ministering in personal prophecy and Recognition of Ministry Gifts and Callings to help Equip the Saints.

Since their marriage, many "DIVINE SUPERNATURAL ENCOUNTERS" have occurred in their lives. Karah's book "God Came Suddenly" will be available in the late fall of 2010. It is about how God supernaturally revealed and brought forth her Boaz. It is truly a marriage created in heaven and worked out on earth.

Other Books:
God Came Suddenly
Seven Realms of the Prophetic
Bible Numbers
Eight Bible Ways to get Healed
To schedule a ministry appointment, prophetic mentoring or to order additional books contact:
WWW.NBSOS.org
New Beginnings School of the Spirit
Donald or Karah Young
P.O. Box 55
Moravian Falls, N.C. 28654
NewBeginningsSOS@gmail.com